LOVE AT THE THRESHOLD

*MOMENTS
MUSINGS
AND REVELATIONS
OF AN UNEXPECTED MYSTIC*

Dina Gregory

COPYRIGHT © 2020 BY DINA GREGORY

www.iamdinagregory.com

All rights reserved.

No part of this publication can be reproduced, or transmitted, in any form or by any means (electronic, mechanical, photocopying, recording, or otherwise) without the prior written permission of the author.

Cover Photos by: Terrence Hamilton

Inside Cover Photos: Fer Juaristi

Wheel of Initiation Image: Kathy Kershaw

ISBN: 9781701122062

Contents

Foreword vii

Note to the Reader xi

Entering the Wheel 18

The South— Getting on the Horse of Intention 44

The West— The Symbolic Death 74

The North— Taking Hold of the Sacred Thread......................124

The East— Initiation and Return Journey.................................167

Afterword..207

Acknowledgments 212

Dedication

To all beings who yearn to love and be loved.

Foreword

Dina is the real deal. She is also, like many progressive thinkers and doers, ahead of her time.

The one word that comes to mind when I think of Dina is "genuine." That in and of itself is a gift to all those who cross her path, as I have, and as you are now in reading her book.

This informal, genuine, quirky and wisdom filled book, that you now hold in your hands (or read on your electronic device) is an authentic expression of one woman's journey toward genuineness.

This book of musings and poetry is her expressed initiation to find the life that fits her. Fits her in a wild, beautiful, sensual way.

Her words will inspire and initiate you, but you must allow her unique approach to the written word in, as is.

She refuses to do things as she *should* and invites you, her reader, to follow your own heart and soul in the pursuit of a truer life, an initiated life.

Her life and writing is not an A-to-B kind of read. So, those of you who want a clear reveal of what to do to awaken to your own personal destiny, you won't find that here.

Dina is crazy-real with her life, her words and her message here.

Read it like you would sit by a sea – there are no rules, no clear path or agenda. There is soul, there is a call to initiation, your own and the planet's.

You ready? Listen.

Listen like you would to ocean waves beat, beat, beating against the shore of our collective soul.

Or, to a sweet chickadee calling out one last time on the brink of sunset.

There's something here for you. If you choose.

Julie Tallard Johnson
MSW, LCSW, author of *Wheel of Initiation*
www.julietallardjohnson.com

There is a sacredness in tears. They are not a mark of weakness, but of power. They speak more eloquently than ten thousand tongues. They are the messengers of overwhelming grief, of deep contrition and of unspeakable love.

—*Washington Irving*

Note to the Reader

When I reflect on the confluence of factors that have brought me to the threshold of birthing my first book, I am reminded that its formation was shaped by a delicate interplay of both internal and social forces.

This book will leave the safety of my womb and be born into a world that is currently polarized by the dualities of "left" and "right" and where the telling of plain and simple truth appears to be a lost art.

While this book is not overtly political in nature, I cannot separate it from the landscape from which it was written. I cannot separate the personal heartbreak expressed in this book from the broken heartedness that I bear witness to in the world.

While the activist in me has felt pulled in a million directions over these past couple of years, I have realized that in times of division and darkness, the most revolutionary act is to remember that you are whole and to dare to shine the light of your soul.

For me, writing thus far has been a tool for coping with life's sorrows and making sense of the world through contemplation. Above all else, it's been a form of emotional excavation and a way of coming to know my true Self.

While I have a loud, gregarious, and humorous personality—complete with a foul mouth, a short temper, and a propensity to cross the line between the sacred and the profane—the truth is that my personality houses a soul that is actually highly sensitive, tender, and shy.

I certainly didn't set out on my journey with the goal of becoming a "mystic". Life simply pressed me in such a way that to not accept this revelation of who I am, would have been a detriment to my becoming.

For a long time, I considered myself to be the spiritual but not religious type. However, when I was working as a teacher at Emma Lazarus High School in New York City, there was something about witnessing the discipline that my Muslim students displayed when they came to my classroom to pray, that instilled in me a desire to find a path that married both my yearning for inner freedom with the discipline required to bring about true and lasting transformation.

Not too long after this desire arose in me, I came across Julie Tallard Johnson's book *Wheel of Initiation*. As both a seeker and a teacher I was drawn to the ways in which she utilized transformational rites of passage for both adults and teens and from the first few pages, I knew she was a woman who walked her talk.

I loved how the Wheel, an ancient template used by many cultures around the world, provided me the freedom to drink from the many wells that bring divine wisdom, while also providing me a compass to navigate my way out of the woods of my soul.

Aside from Julie who acted as my Yoda, I also relied on the spirit of my Nonna, a woman who lived her faith in simple ways and taught me to have a direct relationship with God.

My greatest memories of her consist of those early morning hours when I'd pretend to be asleep just so I could eavesdrop on her muffled petitions to the Blessed Mother.

She died just before I graduated from high school, which in retrospect was my first initiation into the mystery of grief. On the day of her funeral I saw a butterfly flutter over her casket, and it brought to mind a 35-millimeter film we have of my Nonna trying to capture one with a gorgeous smile strewn across her face.

This encounter brought me a momentary sense of peace that sent me on a lifelong journey following the flutters. From staring at the Sistine Chapel, to climbing the hills of Machu Picchu, to getting lost in a Latin lover's eyes from the dopamine highs produced when two beings fall for the same illusion.

After completing my post college backpacking adventure through Central and South America on a trip to "find myself," I moved back in with my parents and not long after met my husband to be.

In 2009 we got married on a beautiful hacienda on the outskirts of San Miguel de Allende, Mexico with about 40 of our closest friends and family. We had no intention of getting married in front of a cross, but when one was so rustically yet elegantly displayed at the center of the hacienda, we figured it would be nice to include it as a token of our Catholic roots.

We were married by a Jewish lay minister and the ceremony we created was a hodgepodge of different cultural rituals, one of which was a Celtic Loving Cup ceremony meant to remind us of both the sweet and bitter moments of life.

My favorite ritual, though, was the balloon release in my Nonna's name. We held it together, said a silent prayer, and then simultaneously let it go. When it got caught on a fence there was a dramatic pause among the guests. Finally, though, it took off to great applause.

As I reflect on my process in writing this book, it feels much like the journey of that balloon. I have been stuck on the fence, frightened of letting go of these pages and revealing my innermost thoughts and feelings with the world.

The truth is that as much as I yearn for the applause that balloon received when it finally took off, I am afraid that after all of this effort in writing this book, its impact may be subtler than my ego's desire for recognition.

I'm afraid that the words that I've held so dear may fall flat or worse, be judged. However, I've finally reached the brink in which there is just simply too much truth living inside of me, and I sense it is time to let it loose.

At several points, I've been asked what the goal of my book is and how I hope it will impact others. At first, I had grandiose visions of my love story becoming the next *Eat, Pray, Love*.

However, the more I pushed this book to serve a particular outcome, the more pain it caused me. This story wouldn't let go of me until I let go of my need to control it. Eventually, I realized that this testimony simply wanted to be given life and the space to unfold and evolve.

As my mentor Julie mentioned in her Foreword this is not a book that is going to tell you in any direct way how to awaken to your personal destiny. In fact, I recommend that you approach this book as a collection of snapshots connected by an invisible sacred thread.

In *Wheel of Initiation,* Julie writes a lot about the Sacred Thread in the North of the Wheel, the direction where we connect with our divine guide/guides and where this invisible thread begins to reveal itself in our life.

With further inquiry, I have learned that many diverse cultures make reference to a thread of life. In an ancient Chinese legend, there is a red thread said to link two people who are destined to be married and in Christianity a "scarlet thread' appears in Genesis and is said to be traceable throughout the Bible.

Given that in my journey I have relied less upon scripture and more upon direct experience, I am not the one to tell you where this thread can be found in and amongst the lives of biblical characters.

However, I can trace this thread throughout my own life, and I have come to understand that though it is invisible to all but me, it is the holiest possession of my life.

In times of uncertainty we want to grasp onto people, places, ideas, and beliefs. I think it makes feel in control. The thought that the lives we planned can be interrupted by life is disconcerting and we begin grasp tighter onto that which we have built our lives on, when in actuality the peace we so long for comes from letting go.

Through loss and deep contemplation, I have come to realize that the only thing worth grasping onto in life is this sacred thread, because it allows those around me to be free.

While I wrote this book first and foremost for my own healing, it is my hope that by sharing these poignant snapshots of my initiatory journey and my longing for true love, that you too will have the courage to cross your own threshold (whatever that may be), the faith to live the questions, and the trust to know that if you seek it wholeheartedly you too will come to discover the thread that connects every joy and every pain of your sacred life.

In releasing these alchemical words, I pull the sword from my heart and promise to my Self from this day forward to fight the good fight with discerning wisdom, humor, laughter, lightheartedness, humility, full creative expression, and most of all—defiant joy!

Dina Gregory

LOVE AT THE THRESHOLD

*

As I dip my pen into the well of Source
I ponder how much power is contained in the written word.
Given the set and setting of our present day,
which makes me feel
as if we are meandering our way through the Book of Revelation
in this collective salvation story
who is it that God wants this character
the world knows as Dina to play?

She certainly won't be that voiceless one from the Bible
Whose story, stifled by patriarchy,
only recounts of her rape.

When I collect the broken pieces of my heart
and put them back as God intended
I wonder if it is you, Lord,
a name I never imagined I'd say aloud,
that acts as the nucleus
from which all parts of me can live peacefully as one,
and if you are,
then tell me who might I become

Will you cast me in the role
of that quirky Mary Poppins-like teacher
who gets her students to believe in the magic
of pursuing their dreams?

But if it's truth that sets us free
better save a seat at your table
for that foul-mouthed comedian
who spits truth like fire
and has an ability
to be both reverent and irreverent
in the same damn breath.

And of course you can't forget

LOVE AT THE THRESHOLD

that sensual, salsa-dancing woman
who can cause quite a storm when she goes ignored
She's so hungry for justice
You'll probably turn her into a diva
to star in the musical of her very own life.

But in this time of so much sorrow and strife
I wonder if you will call upon my inner wise-woman
to show the people where they've gone astray?

Is this what it means to be on the battlefield for my Lord?

Oh but that sweet, innocent
wild child in me doesn't want another war.
No, that fearless little girl
with her snorting laughter
wants nothing more
than for us to settle our conflicts
with a good game
of Capture the Flag,
where we all run through the night
wielding our plastic swords in hand, screaming
"Hasta la Victoria,"
innocence at last!

DINA GREGORY

Entering the Wheel

Give your hearts, but not into each other's keeping
For only the hand of Life can contain your hearts
And stand together yet not too near together:
For the pillars of the temple stand apart,
And the Oak tree and the Cypress grow not in each other's shadow.

—Kahlil Gibran, "On Marriage"

. . . As the sacred rhythms are played on the drums, unspoken stories of injustice begin to slowly traverse their way through the blood in my veins.

I walk over to the window and I see a stink bug trapped between two panes of glass. I stare for a while contemplating if there is any way to free him.

The drums grow louder and suddenly I feel as if I'm trapped. Suffocating oppression without an escape.

An image taken on our wedding day, when blood suddenly began to stream down from my jugular notch flashes before my eyes.

A river running between the banks of my breasts, prefiguring this moment when the pain of an ancient past would come crying to me from the ground.

Injustice wants to be given voice, yet it is caught in my throat. And it makes me feel as if I'm being choked, and *I can't breathe.*

I scream and shake. They try to calm me by fanning me with sage, but I yell at them to go away.

The call for justice is an inconvenient intrusion upon our illusory peace.

I guard my anger like a ferocious tiger, "Don't you dare tell me it has no place here!"

Everyone stares in a pregnant silence.

The self-doubt that has long kept my mouth shut is decimated by this river of rage. Soon enough thunderous truth begins to flow from my mouth.

The bonds of marriage broken, mental slavery cracked open.

ENTERING

Only one dares to challenge my anger. She walks confidently in my direction and demands I clasp her hands.

Her body becomes the machine upon which I place the weight of years of misplaced rage.

She looks deep into my eyes, seeing through me and beyond.

Until rage turns to tears and I find myself
in a pool of sorrow.

"Mercy," I beg.

Upon this plea,
my heart breaks open
and miraculously I am free.

Yet now I know why the caged bird sings.

April 17, 1998

I lived tonight mom.

I was overwhelmed with the dream I was living. Overwhelmed with the potent romance alive in the streets.

Fountains on every corner. The water running off made a small pond on the cobblestone and I saw my reflection and learned so much.

I saw more than just me, but the world around me. I wanted more time to absorb the story behind this classic romance novel.

The story that is told in someone's heart.

I was on top of the world staring over a city that sang to me, making me realize the ingredients that run through my veins that make up my soul, my very being.

I danced tonight mom.

I danced a song that was in my heart. The Eiffel Tower shone bright, casting its light upon the lookout.

I heard the echoes of the djembe drums throughout myself. I felt the embarrassment and fear of others to let their song release from their hearts into their feet, but I was just taken by the rhythms.

I grabbed this man's hand and danced with him in a circle of cheers. Although we could not understand each other, we both knew we had to let ourselves go.

I cried tonight mom.

For some reason of which I am not sure. But I can taste the salty remains that have settled on my face and lips.

They speak more than words.

ENTERING

Everything I hoped it to be, the lights, the cobblestone, the music.

Inside my heart lived me the dreamer, the impulsive spirit, the scared child, and on and on.

For those few moments I had a sense of completeness. My every move spoke to me.

I was you tonight mom.

Thank You.

August 10, 2012

Tonight at the Yoga of the Voice retreat, we honored the men. I thought of you and how much we've grown in the circle of our marriage.

I lie awake now for the first time in years, trying to get out the words to a love song that my heart has longed to sing.

Do you know that when I was a child I used to wake my mother in the middle of the night to write down lyrics to songs that wouldn't let me sleep?

She'd lovingly oblige and scribble down a few lines. To think that we both thought that music was to be made in the next lifetime.

When I met you those bongos were on the top of your bookshelf, your guitar hidden in a closet, my voice locked away in a cage.

I honor you tonight.

> You are my temple.
> You play the music
> that opens the door to my soul,
> creating the space for my voice to unfold.
> Your rhythms stir
> something deep inside me,
> Your melodies
> sweep me off my feet
> and carry me to Heaven.

October 12, 2013

We gather under the shade of the old elm to bless our land. Sheepfold Farm, that's what the former owners called it.

Nervous I question, "Who am I to lead a ceremony such as this?"

I wonder if one needs a title to deem oneself holy?

Doubt subsides, wisdom slowly and steadily arises.

Paloma calls upon the sacred directions.

We honor the Mohican ancestors.

Friends bury crystals, marking the boundaries of the property.

The fire burns, smoke spirals in the air, bansuri flute intermingles with the wind.

> May this land know love.
> May this land know laughter.
> May this land know joy.

Prayers spoken, hearts opened.
You step forth to the center.

Your voice deeper than usual; surely this is the sound of your tribal soul.

You speak and I feel the ground shake. Agua de Florida spouts forth from your mouth:

> *Gracias Madre…Gracias Padre….*
> *Gracias Madre…..Gracias Padre….*

The ceremony is now closed. This land now blessed.

March 31, 2014

Turkey came knocking on our window this morning
Brought a message from high up above.
Says, "You've wrapped love around you like a wild rose bush
it's time to give,
give away,
give away,
your love."

Yesterday we celebrated your birthday, explored the edges of the property as if we were a couple of teenagers again.

We sang in the barn with hay under our feet and I imagined what this place could become: a space for community, ritual, ceremony, and celebration.

Old Dutch farmhouse . . .
Wide plank floors . . .
Exposed beams . . .
Everything we ever dreamed…..

It's a hidden slice of Heaven.
Truly, it is,
the way the old elm frames the Catskill Mountains,
it's bucolic indeed.

May 13, 2014

Alarm sounds.

I groggily make my way to my cushion. Habitual fingers open my email. There's a message from Don. Only one sentence.

>"D—Ceil is dead."

How dare death come without an introduction. There's no, "I'm afraid to say." Just raw death staring me in my face.

I'm lifted from my meditative position. Don whimpers on the phone. Frozen in time among a room of ticking grandfather clocks.

You calmly find my bag and help to order my thoughts. Quietly, I judge your lack of emotion. We drive in awkward silence.

You remind me I need to call out of school; you are the master of tangible things.

Strange, this moment doesn't totally consume me. I notice the man crossing the street and how it angers you that he doesn't hurry his step, even though the light is green.

We cross the Tappan Zee Bridge and I try to recall the last conversation Ceil and I had. It was about Motherhood.

She told me to follow my heart. Yet I'm unsure how to do that with all these voices in my head.

We pull up, and run in. Don is a ghost, face forlorn and in shock from their last kiss, with his lips on hers trying to revive life.

They just celebrated thirty years of marriage.

I can't believe she is gone. They are Ceil and Don.

I can't say one name without the other.

We listened to each other's lives unfold through the old vents of my childhood home.

She was like a second mother, even saved my life when I choked on a Dorito.

I can't believe she has left us with no warning.

He loved her so much.

They were actually smitten with each other.

Oh how he looked at her with those short Bongo jeans, Betty Boop style, and her famous sweet iced tea.

It was as if she were a Queen.

Our love, I'm afraid to admit, is not a Ceil-and-Don kind of love.

I tell you I will stay the whole week to hold space, and be at his side.

You seem perplexed by my choice.

But for the first time in my life there is only one place I yearn to be.

June 16, 2014

I found an English as a Second Language (ESL) teaching job upstate.

It's a mere fifteen minutes from our farm. I was randomly searching for a new job online when I was sitting, bored, at Don's side during the week of Ceil's funeral.

The school is named Ichabod Crane, after that funny schoolteacher in Washington Irving's "Legend of Sleepy Hollow."

Growing up, my friends and I knew that school as the one that closes for even just a few snowflakes.

There is even an Urban Dictionary definition of it.

You can actually "Ichabod Crane" something, which means to cancel something because of weather, even if the weather conditions aren't that severe.

The job is only part-time. Quitting a full-time one doesn't make sense—but I'm tired of making sense.

Life feels too fleeting for it to always have to make sense.

I love my students, but I can't ignore this voice inside that tells me to go.

Is it crazy to think that Ceil is guiding me? That her spirit is leading me to this new life?

I've never even lived alone before, and soon enough I'll be living alone in a house in the woods.

You think it's a bad decision, but I take the job anyway.

I've concocted a plan in which you stay in the Brooklyn apartment while I move to live full-time in our farm Upstate.

I don't see how else we will come to find out if country life is really as romantic as it seems.

We will see each other on the weekends.

But I can see the distance already growing between us and I haven't even left.

You are mad at my decision.

I think you feel like I'm abandoning you, but if I don't go, I'll be abandoning myself.

June 30, 2014

> *I feel it.*
> *I am on the brink.*
> *That instant right before night ends and day breaks,*
> *that moment right before a blossom bursts into a flower.*
> *that tension upon which Creation manifests.*
> *shedding the ways I used to be,*
> *and surrendering to the woman I have yet to become*

We are a small circle of women coming to spend a weekend at the farm, healing and howling at the moon.

One of my friends leads a mini mask painting workshop. I don't think I've done something like this since high school studio art class.

I hated that project. I sat there every day wondering why my mask didn't look like the girl's sitting next to me?

Ms. Straw nudged me to proceed.

I ended up making a blue androgynous face with hair made of grass.

She told me she was proud.

My new mask is purple with an orange spiral tree sprouting from a leaf, which I unevenly glue to the third eye.

There's a green stripe down the center of the nose, and green dots that stem from the brow line shooting out to its temples.

I don't want to admit it, but this is fun. I should put paint on stuff more often.

Flor has prepared a sound bath in the farmhouse basement. As we get ready to start, we hear a noise.

Karina seems to know exactly what it is; she runs to the chimney cleanout door. She says it's a bird.

She confidently opens the door. Out comes flying a mourning dove; it dips and dives, searching for the open sky.

She is sure it's a *dakini*, a word the Tibetan Buddhists use for the female embodiment of enlightenment.

She says it's an omen of good things to come.

We spend the night sharing our stories, shedding our tears.

Topless, we sing and dance as the fireflies light up the night sky.

July 3, 2014

I'm at Karmê Chöling Shambhala Center for a two-week meditation retreat in Vermont.

The teacher is seated in his red chair and his assistant ceremoniously brings him a glass of water.

I like how they place the napkin on the top of the cup with such precision.

Yet, it simultaneously irks me.

"Why the hell is he so special? What does he know that I don't?"

I recall my first meditation class.

I got hooked when the teacher said, "You may never get good at meditation, but you might become kinder to yourself."

I like the idea of kindness. Sitting still and not talking for a week, I'm not sure is for me.

My Finnish neighbors from the farm think I'm crazy.

They can't believe I am actually paying money to be at "silent camp."

My knee begins to shake. I wonder why that teacher's eyes seem so soft.

If only I had that pin he wears on his lapel, perhaps I'd get that serene and spiritual, doe-eyed look.

But that would be at least another five years.

Tick tock tick tock.

I can't stand another second.

A wave of thought and emotion. I hear a cough, a rustle. I start to fantasize.

The man on the cushion in front of me has an Italian last name.

I purposely sat behind him just in case he turns out to be "the one."

A quick judgment.

"No, you're not supposed to do that! Hypocrite! You just told your husband that this is the precise moment couples begin to cheat. And weren't you the one to encourage him to dig deep?"

I wonder what I am supposed to do.

Are all thoughts meaningless, even holy ones?
Or all thoughts holy, even sinful ones?

tick tock tick tock

Another wave. I'm supposed to let it pass but I can't take it anymore.

I need to cry so many tears.

I don't know where life is leading me and I don't know if I'm the one in charge of leading life.

They say this road leads to Shambhala, a mythical kingdom of peace, tranquility, and happiness.

Seems like a far and distant land.

The teacher told us to write down why we have come here.
I write, "I want to experience a sense of fullness from within."

Yet the only thing I feel is full of shit and tears and fear.

Sleeping on the temple floor feels like summer camp.

Not that I actually went to one. But if I did, I imagine it would be like this.

With all these complicated Buddhist teachings that everyone shares at lunch breaks, I find it cute to watch these same people snore.

A tall and handsome spiritual jock has been laying on a mattress inches away from me.

During afternoon walking meditations, I've taken to watching the way in which he slowly places his feet to the floor.

Heel toe, heel toe.

July 10, 2014

There's a thunderstorm that makes me jump from my bed. Spiritual Jock Man stirs as well.

My heart is racing. There is no way I can go back to sleep.

With the pouring rain, I feel a tension growing in the air and wonder if it is just me.

I think of you and how distant you've been acting toward me. Surely there must be another woman by your side.

I pull off my covers and ask if I can crawl into his.

He begins to caress my skin. Soon enough I feel the weight of his body on top of mine.

With the rain pouring down, surely the thirty other people sleeping in this temple won't hear.

This feels dirty, but it shows me I want sex that makes me feel holy.

We stop before we go too far.

The next day I witness seekers taking Refuge vows to the Buddha, the Dharma, and the Holy Sangha.

I think perhaps a year from now I'll be ready to take Refuge vows. But does that mean I'd have to forgo any remaining notions I have of Heaven?

I still cross myself when I am flying high in the sky. And at Christmastime when all the others rush to eat, I'm still the one who insists we say a proper grace.

If not for Jesus, at least for my Nonna's sake.

July 15, 2014

I decide to extend my somewhat silent retreat and call Amtrak's customer service department to change my ticket.

The man on the other end of the line and I get to talking and he asks me why I'm sitting on a cushion for two weeks when all I need is the Holy Spirit.

I laugh.

Could I trade the Father, the Son, and the Holy Spirit for the Buddha, the Dharma, and the Holy Sangha?

At this point, it would be nice if I could simply believe in me, myself, and I.

August 16, 2014

I've come to the Omega Institute to sing in a circle and let improvisation lead the way.

Bobby McFerrin, who taught the world not to worry and be happy, shows us we are human instruments.

With the interplay of melodies, I momentarily forget that it was only six hours ago that my cat took her last breath on that plastic table.

My hand caressing her head.

No more piss stains on the couch, but I miss sweet Tigger's purr.

Breath sound,
sound breath.

There is music in my body and it brings me to my feet.

I see a woman who reminds me of my Aunt Ardie.

Her soft gaze, and her strong yet humble way draws me near and I feel at ease at her side.

I remember Ardie's words on our nuptial day. They were spoken at my parents' wedding too.

"Love one another, but make not a bond of love: let it rather be a moving sea between the shores of your souls."

My eyes well up.

The singing continues. A tear in my mouth, salt on my tongue, a smile breaks through—

I like this circle of human instruments.

ENTERING

I'm an integral part of it.

I feel my breath, the sound of my voice mixing with others and for a brief moment I am taken out of myself.

August 24, 2014

You pull away, on your way back to Brooklyn and here I am, alone in our "dream home".

It's for real. I'm doing this.

I start my job at Ichabod Crane in a few short days and my life as I've known it, is now gone.

I listen till I no longer hear the sound of gravel underneath your tires.

My coldness gives way to tears. Months of anticipation lay heavily on my chest.

Almost a year ago to this day, we spent our first night as the new owners of Sheepfold Farm.

Sitting on this very brick shelf, we drank wine and contemplated the joys and pains this home would come to know.

Little did I think we were sitting on the edge of a precipice.

Who would have thought that I would be the one to choose the woods?

And you, who guided us on a backpacking adventure through the Canyonlands, would have chosen the solidity of concrete?

I step outside in front of our old elm.

I place my bare feet on the ground. Though I can feel them, I have no idea where we stand.

How can this terrible feeling of loneliness give birth to something grand?

September 28, 2014

I got another part-time job working as a migrant tutor. I told you to trust me that things would work out.

In the morning, I am at Ichabod Elementary and in the afternoon I run over to tutor migrant students in the high school.

This tutoring job has got me thinking about my days in college when I marched for farmworker justice and how that experience propelled me to travel through Central and South America where I learned Spanish, fell madly in love, and now…. I'm here.

It's one of those life come full circle moments. I wonder how many of these you get to have in a life time.

Country living is a little strange, the school is so traditional. They actually stop and stand to say the Pledge of Allegiance.

I haven't done that since I was in elementary school.

The teachers bring their lunches to school and there are no more outings to get dollar dumplings on Hester Street.

People are nice, but I feel out of place.

I've got a "too cool for school," I'm from "the city" complex.

My neighbor Brenda who works at the local liquor store is helping me adjust.

She's taken to making fun of me. "Oh you City people . . . come here thinking you are better than the rest of us. Look, City girl is afraid of a cow!"

The other weekend I went to some party for a Democratic candidate, less for politics and more in hope of meeting some like-minded friends.

I bee-lined to a tall gorgeous woman with bright red hair.

Swiss German, divorced with two girls who go to my school.

"Will you be my new best friend?" I ask with no pretense; only loud desperation.

When she has me over, we bond over bottles of wine.
Her farmhouse has a shabby chic and urban flair.

Brazilian jazz plays in the background.

Her eccentric friend recites from Rilke's "Duino Elegies" in a loud, expressive voice.

It pierces me, awakening long suppressed desire.

The South—
Getting on the Horse of Intention

Initiation represents the most significant spiritual phenomena in the history of humanity. It is an act that not only involves the religious life of the individual in the modern meaning of the word "religion" but it involves his whole life.

It is through initiation that in primitive and archaic societies it is how man becomes what he is and should be—a being open to the life of the spirit, hence one who participates in the culture into which he was born. . . . This is why initiation represents a decisive experience for any individual who is a member of a pre-modern society; it is a fundamental existential experience because through it a man becomes able to assume his mode of being in its entirety.

—Mircea Elide, *Rites and Symbols of Initiation*

October 31, 2014

My teacher Julie told me to choose an initiatory intention.

We've settled on, "I live simply."

What kind of intention is that?

Simplicity. That's not for me.

Simplicity is content stacking logs of firewood, but I burn like a wildfire.

"I live simply," I repeat aloud.
"I live simply."

The words begin to settle on my tongue and I actually don't mind the taste of them.

After all, when I live simply, I feel my fingers typing on these keys.

I notice how the dish soap bubbles gather in the drain of the sink.

I can tell when my student has cut her bangs.

Perhaps living simply is the way I awaken to the fullness of my being.

Perhaps living simply is the steady stream of air that keeps the fire burning long into the night.

My resistance subsides.

I decide to plant the seed of my intention . . .

I live simply . . . So be it.

November 25, 2014

I can't sleep. I watch your chest rise and fall wondering how we've gotten here.

Perhaps with the holiday and other people around, I'll get a new vantage point from which to see you from.

I'll watch you and my mother talk about the stuffing. You'll say, "Eight whole onions, really?"

She'll say, "Yes, plus four sticks of butter."

We'll laugh.

I'll tell you that I wore my swimming goggles to stop my eyes from watering.

I roll over and stare at our bedroom fireplace.

 I can't help but wonder who is the woman who keeps you from answering your phone on those awful weeknights when I feel so alone.

Shouldn't you want to call and comfort me, assure me that the noise that makes me jump from bed is just a chipmunk?

But no. There is always some kind of excuse as to why you can't answer your phone.

I can't keep denying this knowing I feel.

Jealousy has the needle of my compass spinning in circles and I don't know North from South.

Where did our love go?

You know the love I found in that temple, when Madrecita lifted the haze of judgments that clouded the way I saw you?

Remember how I screamed and cried when I thought I heard Her tell me you would die?

You ran to me, held my hand, took me outside, told me there was nothing to worry about because you were there by my side.

On the steps, we looked out over the Catskill Mountains and began to dream our farmhouse dream.

You showed me living could be simple and that in spite of all the darkness, pain, and grief, I could just choose to focus on the light.

You pointed out how beautiful it was just to watch the trees sway.

Maybe that is all we need to do.

Sit together and watch the trees sway, until the darkness between us fades away.

THE SOUTH

November 26, 2014

Another sleepless night. I can't take it anymore.

You appear sound asleep. I tiptoe to your nightstand. I must put my mind to ease. I take your phone into the living room.

I find the proof I'm looking for and I feel an unexpected sense of relief.

I return to bed and swallow my pain. At least now I know I'm not crazy.

I don't know how I make it through Thanksgiving.

In between the shuffle of dishes and the laughter of guests I whisper, "Don't leave me."

There is a momentary softness. I take refuge in the warmth of your arms. I tell myself I can just forget what I saw.

Our bellies are now stuffed. You are fast asleep on the floor. My dad yells, "Kids it's time for bed."

Can I swallow my pain for another night?

I breathe heavily. You say, "What's wrong?" I tell you that I know.

We cry on the floor of our walk-in closet where we once did a happy dance.

Life feels so fleeting. The dream we've only just brought to fruition is crumbling before my very eyes.

When that turkey came a knockin' why did I open the door?
Must we break apart to give away our heart?

December 10, 2014

Thud. A cardinal slams into my kitchen window.
 I run outside.

The contrast of this bright red bird against snow-covered grass captures my eyes.

I pick him up in my hands.
He is alive, but dazed and confused.
Much like myself.

Ceil liked cardinals.
She used to feed them outside her bedroom window.
Maybe this is her spirit coming for a visit.

December 27, 2014

If I were in the city with you, tonight we'd be having Indian Monday and Netflix.

Instead, I'm in a dark and lonely house with no neighbor in sight.

Solitude is a funny thing.

When the sun rises I greet the solitude like a dog greets its owner after a long separation.

I welcome being alone with open arms.

I look forward to my morning ritual of watching the spiraling smoke of incense from my meditation cushion.

I do those weird Shambhala Warrior exercises I learned at that Karmê Chöling retreat and in a lunge position I shout at the top of my lungs Ki-Ki-So-So!

I enjoy the space that solitude gives me to read poetry aloud in a dramatic voice with no worry that you might judge the early morning theatrics.

I relish in the ritual of making a cup of coffee, sitting in my corner with my journal in hand, watching the mist rise over the distant mountains.

With time before work, I will even make my way past the ash tree up to the sacred circle that you so diligently keep mowed.

I speak my prayers to the universe. I reaffirm my intention to live simply and to uplift the lives of others by uplifting my own.

This is sacred time, food for my hungry soul.

Being alone at night is different.

Solitude suddenly transforms into utter loneliness. Everyone here retreats to their homes and their evening routines.

There's no buzz of city life, nothing to distract me from the noise inside my head.

Every time I pull up our driveway and see an empty and dark house, fear begins to percolate.

I had no idea that a wide open sky could make you feel like you are suffocating.

I find if I slow my step, and stop myself from running from the car to the front door, the fear begins to subside.

I've taken to humming songs to soothe the scared child inside.

I've wanted to take the time to befriend the dark, to walk around alone at night and explore her mysterious and wild ways.

Yet, I'm afraid to admit I haven't strayed too far from the front porch.

I come inside, lock my door, and soothe myself with a fantasy of the woman I long to be.

She is beautiful and wild and howls at the moon.

But the woman I am now surfs Facebook when the silence becomes too much to bear.

She shuffles papers around helping to create some order out of the mess of her mind.

A little to the right, now a little to the left.

December 29, 2014

We try to give it a go, a weekend away in the Adirondacks.

Right before leaving, I catch a glimpse of an eagle flying above our home.

Pretty sure he's come to tell us that we need a higher perspective.

On our drive to our mountain getaway, we make an impromptu stop at Chapel Pond.

Briefly it feels almost as if we are dating again. You put your hand around my waist. I try to narrate in my head that this is our turning point.

When we get to our bed and breakfast, we unpack our things.

"Listen," I say, "we have nothing to lose; how much worse could it be if we just spoke our truth?"

We draw a bath and lay in the tub, sharing the truth of where it all went wrong.

I realize that this is what it really means to be naked.

I tell you of my suffering from having left my heart on that beach in Viña del Mar.

Perhaps you feel relieved that your jealousy was founded upon truth.

You listen and actually empathize with my pain. You admit that you proposed to me in fear, afraid that after a summer in Spain I'd take a train to Switzerland, in search of a long-lost love.

Had it not been for that diamond ring weighing me down, I think I would have taken that chance.

We talk about the other woman. I ask what needs she fulfills.
You say it feels good to just have someone who seems to like you.

In bed later we make love. I have you call me by her name.

Truth, even dirty ones, seem to turn me on.

Why does no one tell us about this part of marriage?

We decide to go to the brewery to drink some IPAs.

As we drive, I stop to check my phone. There's a message from my colleague. The mother of one of my fourth-grade ESL students is dead.

She is my age. Something with her lungs. She passed on Christmas Day of all days.

I burst into tears. I feel you pull away. I see the shadow of your judgment cast on my heart.

It reminds me of that time we saw that documentary at the Woodstock film fest. *Beyond Conviction,* I think it was called.

Victims brought together with the perpetrators of the crime, for a chance at reconciliation.

I wept nearly the entire time.

There was an image in that film I'll never forget. A woman whose own brother raped her found herself on that precarious edge, the one that forces us to make a choice between holding a grudge or choosing forgiveness.

My heart trembled the entire time. It seemed like an eternity that she stood by his side.

THE SOUTH

And then she did it.

She placed her hand on his shoulder, in a show of tenderness that held all the complexities of life.

The film ended, and the woman next to me asked if she could hug me.

You walked away with a puzzled and annoyed look. You don't have to understand why I cry the way I do.

Just place your hand on my shoulder.
But, you can't.

We drink our beers in silence.

The waves of my emotions are clearly too much,
and you stand rigid upon the shores of my soul.

December 31, 2014

The mantel of our fireplace has ten years of decorations on it. Cute little ceramic couples that some Chinese lady with a fine-tipped marker inscribed with our names.

The first one I bought you was of a couple traveling. She with the luggage and he with a map in his hand. Last year's ornament was of a couple sitting around a fire.

"Our first Christmas at the Farm."

This year's ornament, instead of a couple, I've opted for two cute bears.

I hold them in my hand. I'm not ready to put them away.

I don't want to admit it but I know it is our last one.

Our table is full the way I had always imagined it.

Our goddaughter Siena is seated next to my father.

She demands that you play the drums later for her concert and you lovingly comply.

She then announces to the table that she just lost her tooth.

My father looks at her and says he just did too.

I guess this is the circle of life.

I stare off at the painting of my childhood home, remembering the sounds that would come from that kitchen.

1,000 pounds of harmony between my whole family.

My dad and Uncle Joey competing for center stage.

My Nonna and my great Aunt Tess harmonizing . . . I go to the bathroom to cry.

If I can only relish this moment with all my being, then perhaps I can honor the fact that dreams, even briefly lived, really do come true.

January 4, 2015

Alvaro.
Mi potro Viejo.
Mi Chileno.

I thought I'd let you go many times before. Not even a one-carat diamond ring could help me forget that simple band made of coconut.

It sits in a three-legged porcelain box in the back of my dresser drawer.

I remember the day I took it off of your hand and placed it onto mine.

Tania, your *gran amor* as you called her, had the other one, but she threw it in the ocean one day when you had a fight.

I took it as a sign that the ring was meant for me and that our love was divine.

For years I swore you were nothing but a distant memory, but that was a lie.

It's clear now. I've spent my marriage with one foot in, one foot out, and as real as our love felt, the truth is that you are nothing but a ghost lover who continues to haunt my mind.

I've been trapped in that dreamcatcher I bought for you that Christmas when your mother, Ofelia, told me that I was an angel sent by your father from the other side.

Alvaro.

You were my Don and I thought I was your Ceil.

THE SOUTH

I'll never forget that afternoon when your uncle said I looked at you as if you were *un pollo rico con papas fritas*.

I tried to convince myself that my love for you had run its course.

But whenever I'd hear our song, I'd *sail away* with the winds of fantasy.

> *Sail away with my honey*
> *I put my heart in your hands*
> *Sail away with me*
> *What will be will be*
> *I want to hold you now, now, now*

A one-month love affair that has played on repeat for ten years.

TEN YEARS!!!!!

But today I release you . . .

I grieve a love that never had its chance to fall from grace.

I release the memory of the way my eyes met yours on the beach in Renanca.

I release the way we dove carelessly in the frigid ocean, drying ourselves, and taking the bus to eat lunch with your Tia Buena Tela.

I release the words of Pablo Neruda, and the way we danced in the street to the music we heard in our hearts.

I release . . .

I release . . .

I release the way we made love of a different kind, that night when all you touched was my heart.

I release the memories of being in your arms as we listened to the songs of Gypsy Kings, Joss Stone, and David Gray.

I release.

I release the comfort of sitting by your mother's side, drinking tea, eating pan con palta, and talking about life.

I release the moment when we made love, wrapped around each other's bodies, eyes open and tears rolling down our faces.

To think that we thought we had found home in the other...

I release . . .

I release the time we drank wine out of a box, sitting on the banks of Rio Valdivia.

I release our dream of a *casa de campo*, on the hill in Niebla, in the special spot we christened on sweating knees.

I release the adrenaline of hitchhiking to Chiloe, watching you dance the Cuenca, waiting for a friendly passerby to stop and give us a ride.

I release . . .

I release the moment that you bid me farewell, at the bus terminal, and the way you tipped your cap as the bus pulled away.

I release all the fantasies about the way our story would end, because I know there is a story I still have yet to truly live.

February 11, 2015

Lady Luna
guide my wild woman spirit
tame her
show her to trust the seasons

In the cold of winter's night
let her know that the warmest place
is to go deep inside

Show her how to gather her energy
to nourish herself from the inside out
as daylight breaks
I know there will come a day
when she will rise

February 14, 2015

I'm desperately grasping onto the picture I have created in my head of my life.

Sunkissed, wavy hair. A polka-dotted dress that hugs the curves of my body. My hand caressing a rounded belly, feeling new life.

I am dancing in the open fields relishing in witnessing the satisfaction my ginger-bearded husband receives from stacking logs of wood one by one by one.

"This is how it's supposed to be!" I protest, digging my heels into the ground, refusing to surrender my position.

But the more I dig the heavier my heart becomes.

Ten years ago it started as a whisper. Easy to cover up with the daily routines of life, adventures, and plans for a distant future.

But now that the future is our present, the whispers of doubt have caught up with us and we finally admit to each other that we jointly collaborated in uniting our fears instead of our hearts.

And now we must be diligent, and discern between the sadness of letting a relationship built on half-truths go . . .

. . . and a real love that beckons us to stay.

But what if it's not the relationship that has to go, but the notions we've held of it?

Can we unravel this knot of fear that we have collaborated in creating?

Can we not fall victim to our mind's habitual ways of making our present about reliving the past?

Can we learn to see each other not through our clouded lens of interpretation, but as we actually are?

The pit in my stomach tightens again.

"But he keeps you at arm's length," an inner voice pleads. "You want someone with whom you can burn wildly like a fire merging together into infinite vastness."

Is this passion I yearn for what draws the moth to the flame?

Is it what will bring about my destruction, or what will bring about my resurrection?

I flip-flop again and wonder if that kind of passion is sustainable.

When you pack a stove so tight with no space for the fire to breathe, it goes out.

Perhaps there is some wisdom in the space we have created and if we sit in it past the point of discomfort, we will emerge transformed.

Do we let go or do we let *be?*

February 21, 2015

The snow is falling and I almost don't make it home.
I slowly take the turn of our driveway,
avoiding the edge of the ravine.
Yet, I'm not sure how much longer I can avoid this edge of my life.

You are cooking us an anniversary dinner.
Duck over a creamy polenta.
Candles are lit.
We are efforting at romance,
but the frigid chill between us still remains.

April 3, 2015

We have separated . . .

So dramatic that line is standing on its own. Am I writing these words, or have they already been written?

I feel like I am turning the pages in the book of my life, but there is no back cover to read to find out how my story ends.

We have separated . . .

The starkness of those words say, "This is where you are, the chapter of your life where all that seemed solid and secure is no longer that way."

A reality I'd rather not accept.

I vacillate between the poles of worry and fantasy, and get lost in weaving stories spun of hope and fear about how it will all work out in the end.

But what end?

What does "it working out" even mean?

Does it "work out" when we get everything we want?
Does it "work out" when there is a certain amount of money in the bank?
Or when the house is painted the right shade of yellow and the next project is complete?

Life is strong-arming me into presence and the beauty of reality is revealing itself.

We have separated . . .

We don't know what comes next, but if I let go of the need for an outcome, I'd see that this moment right now is my happy ending, and *this* moment is my happy ending, and *this* one too.

Perhaps happily ever after isn't the moment when the Prince kisses his Bride.

It is in the acceptance of the groundlessness and uncertainty of life.

Thoughts of the future sneak into the present.

I wonder if one day we will sit here again reunited as husband and wife or maybe as friends, and recollect this moment when life urged us to move beyond our comfort zones.

To grow, it seems we must be willing to die.

I must become the warrior who jumps off the edge of the cliff in trust that there is a net below to catch her.

Ki-Ki-So-So!

April 12, 2015

We are reading *Tiger Rising* by Kate Dimilo in my ESL class. It's about a boy named Rob who encounters a real tiger in a cage in the woods, and his relationship with a girl he meets named Sistine Bailey.

Walking through the misty Florida woods one morning, twelve-year-old Rob Horton is stunned to encounter a tiger—a real-life, very large tiger—pacing back and forth in a cage. What's more, on the same extraordinary day, he meets Sistine Bailey, a girl who shows her feelings as readily as Rob hides his. As they learn to trust each other, and ultimately, to be friends, Rob and Sistine prove that some things—like memories, and heartaches, and tigers—can't be locked up forever.

I showed the class a picture of the Sistine Chapel so they'd know where her name came from.

They were really excited when I told them I had seen it once with my very own eyes.

God giving life to man.
Adam and Eve.
Rob and Sistine.
You and me.

The kids don't know it, but I alternate between trying to find myself in this book and in their eyes.

If there is no back cover to my life, maybe there is a clue on these pages or within these four walls.

It's clear you are Rob and me Sistine.

It's like those therapy sessions we did; I am the tiger and you are the turtle.

When the little girl in me feels afraid, she pounces, fights, and screams just to remain in connection.

And you, just like a turtle you retreat into your shell, overwhelmed by my expression.

We are supposed to learn how to lean into each other.

You are supposed to learn how to express, and me to contain.

I just want you to see that under all of my anger and rage is a scared little girl afraid of her own shadow.

…I love watching my students talk about the book.

The look in their eyes when they discover "Aha Moments" and "Words of the Wiser."

I lose myself in being a spark of their curiosity, wonder, and awe.

But when I return home, I can't help but to feel that tiger pacing back and forth inside the prison of my mind.

Who holds the key to the freedom I seek?

April 17, 2015

It is the first time I am celebrating my birthday without you by my side.

You are off in the wilderness on a vision quest and I'm trying to find a way to not get so distracted that I forget the artichoke dip cooking in the oven.

You are much better about managing things. Somehow you can just get it all done while I whimsically flutter about.

I thought that is what made us a good team. It's hard to be both you and me.

Logic and thoughtful planning seem beyond my abilities. But somehow I magically manage not to burn anything and still mingle with my guests.

I gather everyone in a circle outside. Sara, a girl I am meeting for the first time, smudges everyone with palo santo.

I confess to everyone that you are away and that our marriage is on the rocks. I give thanks for the unknown space between us, and share with my guests my intention to fully and unabashedly be true to myself.

My mom has given me a gift of her favorite songs handwritten in her beautiful Catholic girl script.

She says they are the songs that make up the soundtrack of her life. I like the Frank Sinatra and Jobim song "The Wave" and that line that says:

> *The fundamental loneliness goes whenever two can dream a dream together.*

She's also included Billie Holiday's "Glad to Be Unhappy," Chris Connor's "Blame It on My Youth," Chet Baker's "I Get Along

Well Without You Very Well," and Tony Bennett's "How Do You Keep the Music Playing?"

When I read the lyrics I realize that I'm not alone. I think I'm actually just growing up asking the same questions that every other man and woman alive has ever asked.

How do you make the music last?
How do you lose yourself to someone and never lose your way?

I asked my guests to bring poems and songs to share. My new friend Ana Maria that I met at Spotty Dog Books and Ale shares a Marianne Williamson poem.

I cry when she reads the line: *"Our deepest fear is not that we are inadequate. Our deepest fear is that we are powerful beyond measure. It is our light not our darkness that most frightens us,"*

Is that really true?
Why on earth would I be afraid of my own light?

When all the guests leave, I curl up alone in our bed. Lyrics in hand, I sing myself to sleep.

I get along without you very well
of course I do
except when soft rains fall
and drip from leaves, then I recall
the thrill of being sheltered in your arms
of course I do.

May 11, 2015

I used to be afraid of my own company.
Scared that in the quiet of the night,
I wouldn't like the sound of my own breath.
But here I am
breathing on my own
shedding layers of selves that I've outgrown
like that snake I once saw
who slithered himself out of old skin.

May 31, 2015

I'm at the Stephan Bodian retreat at the Garrison Institute. We are all in a circle.

I like this man. He isn't sitting in some fancy chair that separates him from us.

He is very much a part of our circle, sharing in our humanity. I flip open his book that I have yet to read called *Wake Up Now*.

A quote catches my attention:

> *The Mind is constantly trying to figure out*
> *What page it's on in the story of itself.*
> *Close the book, burn the bookmark.*
> *End of story. Now the dancing begins.*

Anyone that tells me to burn the book and just dance certainly seems to be on to something.

He seems to think we don't need to spend our lives trying to be spiritual, when we already are.

This feels refreshing. I guess I wasn't committing a meditation sin when I'd sneak into the garden to sing and chat with my friend.

Though I must admit I'd still like to know what page I'm on.

He shares a quote from the Gospel of Thomas, "If you bring forth what is within you, what you bring forth will save you, if you do not bring forth what's in you, it will destroy you."

> Bring forth what?
> What is it that this smile of mine hides?
> What is in all these tears I cry?
> How do you bring forth something that you don't even know?

June 3, 2015

"You complete me." Marriages built on movie lines.

We find ourselves yearning to leave because what we have isn't good enough. Greener pastures we are told are somewhere or with someone else because on our own we are never enough.

Soon enough the battle between head and heart ensues. But what if I stop fearing that I made the wrong choice?

What if I could trust that what has kept us together all these years is actually love?

Oh, but you are far too wise. There is a knowing deep inside you, that there are still lessons to be learned.

A premature reconciliation before truly letting go would only serve to sow the seeds of future resentment.

I've mistaken you for the source of my good. No wonder your love couldn't satiate the size of my appetite.

It's simple. We can't choose a relationship before we've chosen ourselves.

You can't fill that hollow space in me, for in it lives the mystery.

The movies have us thinking that the adventure begins when we leave our lives behind, but I choose to put two feet for once in one boat and meet temptation head-on.

The strength of our character will be tested to see if we will persevere.

Can we be patient enough and discerning enough to summit this mountain of conscious love?

The West—
The Symbolic Death

Modern romance, like Greek tragedy, celebrates the mystery of dismemberment, which is life in time. The happy ending is justly scorned as a misrepresentation; for the world, as we know it, as we have seen it, yields but one ending: death, disintegration, dismemberment, and the crucifixion of our heart with the passing of the forms that we have loved.

—Joseph Campbell, *The Hero with a Thousand Faces*

June 4, 2015

You are missing at the dinner table and yet if you were here, you'd still be gone.

The truth is that I miss the company of a man I am yet to meet.

Who is he?

Loneliness rests on my shoulder. I stroke its face.

It asks, "Who are you when you don't have your mirror? Without the beloved to see you, how are you to see?"

The truth, it stings.

I try to comfort myself with the fantasy that we are soon coming to the bend in our road.

What audacity I've had to hope, when hope, too, can be an illusion.

The truth, it stings.

I want to see reality stripped of all hope.

I want to see reality for what it is, and not for how I yearn for it to be.

You don't call, you don't write, you hear my words as demands.

My attempt to connect brings you an onslaught of "I shoulds" and you freeze, not knowing what to do.

The truth, it stings. It is time to take the lessons learned and move on.

Plant seeds of love in fertile soils.

June 28, 2015

I'm returning to Hudson on a Metro North train.

I sit next to an Iranian conceptual artist in search of an eighteenth-century frame.

A delay. A question. A placing away of gadgets. A conversation ensues, smiles exchanged. A connection.

A sandwich and some IPAs. A discussion of beauty and the art of life in motion.

An ice-clinking glass of scotch. A change in body language.

A sharing of beliefs and the stories that we take ourselves to be.

A return ticket changed for the later train. A walk in the rain.

A stop at a frame store to meet the intended goal of the day.

A visit to my parents' house.

A sharing of family stories while jazz plays in the background.

A day like this was not a part of my plan.

I watch closely as he lights my mother's cigarette.

There are laughs and some tears. We pretend we are in the French countryside.

He says he likes the concept of family. I want so badly to be inside his mind.

We linger behind. He grabs my hand.

We sneak in a soft kiss in the hallway.

He's got an 8:40 p.m. train to catch.

I tipsily drive him in my father's beat-up Crown Victoria.
We arrive with ten minutes to spare.

He presses me against my father's car. I'm like a naughty teenager again.

We part ways. I take a last glance at the man with the frame.

I imagine the day it hangs in some SoHo gallery with an Andy Warhol print and the word "human" etched in braille.

It seems we must feel our way back to being human again.

July 26, 2015

On the sacred mound is the skeleton of a bull head and I wonder if this is the place I've come to die.

I place my engagement ring and wedding band on the mound with a rose quartz in the middle, praying that love can somehow heal this divide.

I throw tobacco in the fire.

"For the best of all involved," I pray.

We enter into the womb. I like the sound of the dried sage sizzling on hot grandfather rocks.

The water is poured, steam rises, sweat beads down.

Our elder leads us in singing a Navajo song.
He tells us that in English it translates to "All is well."

Those words are like a sword through my heart.
We contemplated renaming our farm "Allswell."

I pictured it in my mind with a perfect wooden sign.
I want to scream at the sky! Why, God, why?

"Door!"

The sweat lodge door opens and fresh air whips in.

We pray and I cry out my regrets. Your silence has forced me to listen and I don't like what I hear.

Our elder comes around with water. I drink from a wooden cup.

He asks me if anyone has recently died. I imagine he is referring to Ceil.

He says he sees alcohol, a dead baby. Asks if I've ever been pregnant or had an abortion.

I don't think he sees me. I think he sees my mother.

If all he sees is her, then Who AM I?

It's clear we have yet to truly cut the umbilical cord.

Is this what happens when you allow the deferred dreams of your mother to be lived through you?

He sits me in front of the fire and tells me to give it all to the flames.

He says it can handle all of my pain.

How is it possible that I feel even too much for this fire?

He tells me I must let go and stop blocking what wants to come through.

Whatever it is terrifies me. But even if I wanted to feign control, I couldn't.

Great Spirit has brought me to my knees and surrender seems to be my only escape.

July 27, 2015

I have to drive my mother to the doctor.

A car. What is that? A heavy metal object juxtaposed against a veil so thin, I feel as if I barely exist. I tell my mother to hush. She thinks I've gone crazy.

I raise my hand as if a shield. "No!" I *am* fragile. Thirty-four years old and I can feel my soft spot. "Please don't be afraid." I feel her fear encroaching upon me and I'm scared it will lead me to go insane.

"Trust me," I beg. "I need you like I never have before. Please only love, no fear."

She complies though I know it hurts her to see her baby girl this way.

I somehow maneuver this heap of metal to and from the dentist's office and we arrive safely at home and sit in the car.

I beg of her to tell me everything that she knows.

"Tell me about dead babies."

She tells me my great-grandmother lost five, leaving her with twelve. She tells me of Aunt Laura, the one I remind her of who, every time it thundered, used to scream, "San Giovanni Bautista!"

My mother is sweating now.
Truth flows like water on grandfather rocks.

I feel broken. I've opened up a channel of ancestral pain that feels like it's never going away.

I've heard that some Native Americans say that our actions affect the seven generations both before and ahead of us.

The chains of addiction, shame, regret, and limiting beliefs that run in my ancestral line have seemed to accumulate in my very own womb . .

I drop my mother off at home, and return to our farm.

I promise her that I can handle this on my own. I need to be alone. But, I'm frightened.

As I sit in the hammock I suddenly hear a car pulling down our gravel driveway.

It's Marie Claude. I didn't tell her to come, I just warned her that I needed a friend to be on call.

She's carrying flowers. My heart melts. I fall into her arms.

We walk into my living room. I huddle in a fetal position on the living room floor.

She drums and sings and asks me where it hurts. I hold the left side of my womb.

Is this what it is like to give birth?

I dreamt of having a home birth.

You would calm me with the sweet melody of your charango, look at me with reverence, and when that baby let out its first cry it would break open our hearts

And yet here I am, without you, breaking apart.

Marie Claude has me repeat "I am the violet flame, I am the violet flame" over and over again.

I do so until my tears turn to laughter. She bathes me in flowers and tucks me into bed.

July 31, 2015

Lady Luna.
I called out to you in the cold of winter
to tame my wild woman spirit.
You have shown me that the way out is in.

On this warm July summer night,
I seduce you with my dance.
But I'm telling a half-truth.
My words speak of the fruition of my path.

I am not there yet.
I am writhing in the struggle to see the light.
The truth is that I dance to the music given to me by another man,
rather than to the music of my own beating heart.

Life-force pulsing through me.
Help me channel this energy into a deep passion for life.
Ground me in my sensuality,
so that the light of Heaven
can be felt here on Earth.

August 2, 2015

I am a woman who has yearned to see herself through the reflection of another's eyes and I've been drowning in a murky lake of external validation.

No wonder when I held your gaze so tightly your eyes turned black and our love connection broke.

It seems I'm having an unrequited love affair with Self. Yearning to be wrapped up, tied up, and tangled up in Her web.

Your resistance has left me with no mirror. I'm learning to see by listening.

Forced silence makes it impossible to ignore the messages in the Great Conversation between the seen and unseen.

Spirit speaks, when our ears are not clogged with the wax of the world's opinion of us.

Spirit speaks to us in passing moments . . .

We tune in, but then we choose to tune out, for an angel's song on Earth is almost too much to bear.

We forgo the wild chaos of a marriage between Heaven and Hell.

But I choose to be the tree whose roots sink deep down into the Earth with branches that reach for the limitless sky.

August 12, 2015

Ten years came and went. Did you ever think you'd find your wife on match.com? My name was Chispa417, Spanish for spark, and yours was BYY05, best year yet.

My quote was "Gather today the roses of life."

I first heard that quote from my high school French teacher.

It sounds better in French: *Cueillez dès aujourd'hui les roses de la vie.*

Yours was "Experiences are better when shared."

I remember when I met you at the clock in Grand Central.

I didn't like your shirt. It was one of those short-sleeved collared ones made of a heavy cotton with horizontal stripes, which I didn't find too appealing.

But there was something in your smile.

We headed off to St. Marks Place in the East Village. I ordered a Xingu Brazilian beer with that treacle of anise.

There was no, "So, what do you do?" We immediately began sharing stories of our adventurous world travels.

We seemed to just miss each other during our stays in the land of Pura Vida.

I guess we are both wanderers in search of ourselves.

Remember when I laughingly touched your leg and let my hand linger? That's when we knew it wasn't a "just a drink" date.

We proceeded to dinner across the street at an Italian restaurant named Paprika.

THE WEST

When I went to the bathroom you so classily took care of the bill. I was certain that I had found myself a real man.

We left and I could no longer take the pretense of my heels, so I quickly switched them out for flip-flops I'd packed in the bottom of my purse.

It was clear we didn't want the night to end. We took the train uptown to the East Side of Central Park and meandered our way to the West Side.

We shared a kiss that hot humid night leaning on the scaffolding of my friend's apartment building and now ten years later, here we are.

Just waking up from our hazy dream. So quickly we jumped to possess rather than allow the truth of our connection to unfold.

Seemingly overnight, you and me became a "We."

Your white walls soon got a coat of bright-colored paint and we had one of those movie-scene moments where you painted our names on the wall in a heart.

I think my high school boyfriend and I did the same.

The problem was that there was no freedom in our togetherness. Over time we slowly became the projections of the other. You, cold. Me, mean. Problem was, we couldn't clearly see.

There were moments in these years when the haze of judgment lifted and the rays of our beings warmed the garden of each other's souls.

Yet it seems there just wasn't enough sun to sow the seeds of our love.

So this day that I fantasized about reuniting in conscious love, we spend alone.

September 27, 2015

I stand under the light of the blood moon
and I give into the discomfort of shedding this skin.

I choose to flow with the rivers of change.
As the moon turns dark,
I see the light within.
This blood moon reflects the fire,
that I've longed to ignite.

I let go of the old,
to make room for the new.
My head up, my heart open to receive all of me.
In love, in light, in radiance, and in dignity.

October 31, 2015

I stand at the threshold
carrying the weight of a love that has gone wrong
possibly just wrongly interpreted
but I'll never know till I truly let go.
Standing here with my insides shaking,
I decide to finally lay this marriage down to rest.

At this threshold, I lay down
the chains that bind us by duty, fear, and comfort,
the project of prying hearts open
while ignoring my own heart's desires.

At this threshold, I lay down
my demands of you,
my judgment and my blame,
my attempts to push and convince.

At this threshold, I lay down
my grief of letting go of a dream I thought I wanted
and all of the efforting
that I deemed that love required.

As I prepare to cross this threshold
I take in sight the vision of the Great Eastern Sun,
the direction of Spirit's path
and although the path isn't quite clear, I trust it is there,
I trust that in this fall
I'll be caught by God's grace.

I prepare to take the most frightening step,
the next one
where my boat is cut from its moors
and I'm left to drift away at sea . . .

Venturing into the Great Unknown
where dreams that I may never have conceived of are born.

THE WEST

Darkness surrounds,
I find that the lighthouse is within . . .

Crossing this threshold lies freedom,
crossing this threshold I will find love.
Love not dressed in illusion;
love after love.

November 7, 2015

My teacher Julie has given me a spiritual name. Blue Winged Woman.

I like the sound of it. She even wrote me a poem. I can't get the image out of my head.

>*Blue wings over moving water*
>*iridescent silent flight*
>*ready to dive*
>*leaning into earth*
>*water*
>*wind*
>*and fire*
>
>*Blue medicine Buddha*
>*winged in word and deed*
>*her winged body*
>*knows*
>*home*
>*shores beyond view*
>*flies east*
>*creating*
>*a blue shadow light on our world*

My own mother has given me a name as well. I mean after all; she did give birth to me.

She has decided upon "Star Dancer."

My mother writes: "*Dina belongs to no tribe. Rather she joyously dances from star to star to bring each one a little more happiness.*"

She knows me so well . . .

Fiercely independent, joyful, and free; Blue Winged Star Dancer, that's who I'll be.

November 9, 2015

I find change both painful and invigorating.

As I pack the last of my things and ready myself to leave our beloved farm, I catch a glimpse of a bobcat prowling our property's edge. I think he's come to teach me the way to hunt down elusive dreams.

I say good-bye to the sacred circle and to the fire pit where my girlfriends and I sang to the fireflies that lit up the night sky.

I drive up a new gravel road. Up the hill just beyond the railroad tracks to an orange house by the side of the road.

I never would have imagined myself living in a Quaker Intentional Community, but as independent as I want to be, the truth is that I crave community.

When I park my car and take a look at my new home, I recall a moment before I made this move upstate.

I was somewhere in the Bronx grading the English Regents literary responses.

Their essays were based on the poem "The House by the Side of the Road" by Sam Walter Foss.

There are hermit souls that live withdrawn
In the place of their self-content;
There are souls like stars, that dwell apart,
In a fellowless firmament;
There are pioneer souls that blaze the paths
Where highways never ran—
But let me live by the side of the road
And be a friend to man.

Sheepfold Farm was far from being a house by the side of the road, tucked away up a quarter-mile long driveway on a dead-end road.

I guess I don't have a hermit soul.

There are days when passion runs so strong that I'm quite sure I'm one of those pioneering souls, but who knows?

Perhaps I too am meant to live in a house by the side of the road and be a friend to man.

There is laundry drying in the noontime sun and it reminds me of the days I'd spend at my Nonna's window in Queens watching the laundry sway and hearing the planes landing at JFK.

A community of seekers welcomes me, prepared to hold my broken heart in the light.

November 16, 2015

I'm at my special rock, the one that Jens says marks the midpoint of this land, when I get a message from my mother.

They have taken my father to the hospital.

I should have known when he called in a panic telling me that I needed to get home because of the terror attack in Paris.

I had heard this type of fear in him before, but I tried to brush it off.

Last time this happened, Hurricane Irma was on her way. Don found him in a car recording every sound, trying to get it all down.

They took him to the hospital; called it a "manic break."

They say with initiation comes more tests. I thought I'd at least have a chance to rest, but who am I kidding?

This is the circle of life. Every end a new beginning; every turn a new test.

Did I really think I was signing up for comfort when I made my initiatory vow?

This, after all, is the warrior's path.

At the hospital, he pulls me close to him and tells me that everyone is an actor. "Be careful Dina. Don't let them block the exits."

He's watched too much TV. Terror has entered his soul. I grab his hand and I take notice of his barnacles, which is what my family refers to as age spots.

One of the aides is assigned to sit by his side. Every time he panics, she patiently reminds him that "all is well."

I wonder why so many people must reach their breaking point, just to get a witness.

No one can calm him down the way I do. Perhaps this is just too much for his conscious mind.

The Paris attacks happened on the anniversary of the day his son Little Victor was born. Three days later my father watched his baby boy die. He didn't cry, and was angered by my uncle's dramatic Sicilian wailing.

The doctors come and go without taking the time to look deeply into his eyes. They want to slap a label on what appears to be a human experience.

My diagnosis for my father is that life, love, mortality, and unprocessed grief have all caught up with him.

How else would a man of the age of eighty-six, staring down the end of time and lacking the words to express that gnawing feeling inside, cope.

I sing to him about the "Girl from Ipanema," and we laugh, remembering the moment we walked down the beach, and that beautiful goddess passed us leading us both to hum that song in unison . . .

> *When she walks, she's like a samba*
> *that swings so cool and sways so gentle that*
> *when she passes, each one she passes goes ahhh . . .*

Like father like daughter. But there he goes again.

"Dina, where is your mother? She is in danger."

"No, Dad, she is safe at home."

I hold his hand and tell him to breathe. I know the power of our mind to make illusion seem like reality.

One time after consuming too many mushrooms, in a fit of paranoia, I hallucinated that a black man was coming to kill me.
It was my end. I've never screamed so loud in my life. It took three grown men to stop me from running, but there was nowhere to go;

You can't run from your own shadow.

The aide joins me on the empty bed and we sit watching my dad. I ask her if she minds if I share a song.

I sing *Ho'oponopono*. I heard it at a ceremony once. It's a Hawaiian practice of forgiveness and reconciliation.

I was told that *Ho'oponopono* is a ritual that restores and maintains good relationships among family members and with their Gods or God by getting to the causes and sources of trouble.

Ho'oponopono. Ho'oponopono. Ho'oponopono.
Ho'oponopono. Ho'oponopono.
Ho'oponopono. Ho'oponopono.
Ho'oponopono.
I love you
I am sorry
Please forgive me
I thank you
I love you
I am sorry
Please forgive me
I thank you

The song ends and we sit in a luscious silence that makes those beeping machines just another musical texture.

In spite of all the chaos I feel connected to my dad like I've never been before.

I wonder if he thinks everyone is an actor—because life itself is merely a stage.

It's hard to leave him in the hospital, but I must rest. He is safe.
I pull up to the local bar; I'm running on fumes.

He calls me in a panic again, "Dina—the ambulance is at the apartment and they can't get in and your mother is dead."

I'm tempted to drive there but I say, "I'm sorry, Dad. She is fine. We must trust."

If I am wrong I have decided I will forgive myself. I can't live like this. I have feared the day they will pass for so long.

Perhaps I'll be there holding their hands, singing them into the Promised Land. Or perhaps they will die alone the way Ceil did.

I can't control when death calls.

I leave him and drive to the Chatham Brewery.

I order a Bratwurst at the bar. I tell the grease-laden men who spent the day working on cars that I'd like to just listen to their conversation.

Carburetor. I like that word. I want to relish in tangible things made of iron and metal. I find it soothing.

The man without a tooth tells me he'll pray for me.

I'm torn about if I should go to school or call out and be with my father.

I call you and you tell me it is important to sustain a sense of normalcy, that he is safe in the hospital.

I can't tell if you are being cold or if life calls for this type of clear-cut logic. I listen to your advice.

The next day at school my sweet student Nayelli has a gift for me. I open my hand and she places in it an Eiffel Tower charm.

Surely she hasn't seen the news; how can she know?

As I roll it around in my hand, I'm reminded of my sixteenth birthday in the City of Lights and I can't help but think this is some sign.

I run to Ms. Scalzo's room to cry. She tells me she'll pray to her favorite Saint, the Little Flower.

I get a call. Now my mother is in the hospital. She is okay; they think it's just stress.

Math teacher tells me I can handle this—his soft and trusting gaze makes me feel like I can take on the world.

November 18, 2015

We have a divorce mediation session scheduled. It is quick. Not much to be negotiated.

We are told that when we are ready, all we have to do is bring our mediation contract to a lawyer who will file it with New York State.

Neither of us are quite ready to make it that official.

You leave for some ceremony. I get into my car and cry. Why don't you know that this is the ceremony? Life is the goddamned ceremony.

I go to the hospital to see my parents. I'm split between the second and third floor.

Mother Earth and Father Sky.

In a world full of metaphor, I wonder if this is Creator telling me that somehow it is my job to bridge the divide.

I collapse.

I remember this image from a dream. The nurses run to me. "Do you need oxygen?"

"No! Fuck! Someone has to be strong!"

The nurse wipes snot from my nose. I crack a joke, and we laugh.

Luckily Don has come to sit by my side.

The next day, my family comes to the hospital. Uncle Joey tells stories in the lounge. We bond with the couple from Brooklyn, and exchange recipes.

I'm happy and angry and I'm sad.

I wanted these stories to be told around our farmhouse table.

I wanted it to be like my childhood again gathered in the kitchen, harmonizing songs, and playing that crazy Italian card game.

Now my father sits in his hospital gown, holding court. His face is furrowed—he is here but he's in another world.

I want him to be at peace. I want the fear to be expelled from his being. I want to come home and find him listening to jazz with an ice-clinking glass of scotch.

As I look at him in his hospital gown, I don't see a man with some DSM label.

I see a man who draws outside of the lines: an intuitive artist, an unlikely problem-solver with a tough exterior and a tender heart.

Turns out, I am my father too.

December 18, 2015

I'm in the Crandell Theatre in our little town of Chatham. There is nothing that quite screams the winter blues like sitting alone in a theater watching *La La Land*.

Makes me wonder if that jazz composer and drummer I've been seeing off-and-on is "the one." I love how dedicated he is to his craft, and how he really doesn't give a crap about what anyone thinks.

His soft heart revealed only in his music.

He tells me I live by too many rules, trying too hard to please others rather than giving in to what feels good.

For so long we've been told not to trust the flesh. But if I can't trust my own flesh, how will I ever come to trust God?

Maybe there is more wisdom in my body than all the knowledge I seek in books.

He tells me I don't belong in a box. I think he is right. He says I remind him of Janis. The thought makes me smile. Wouldn't it be nice to spend your days singing about the joys and pains of life

Ryan Gosling and Emma Stone dance across the screen,
and my heart flutters.

If only life were a musical where everyone knew the words.

This movie's got me thinking about the way people stumble into our lives. Perhaps he isn't in my life for an ivory romance, but to edge me along in the pursuit of forgotten dreams.

Not too long ago I sat on his living room floor, wearing his button-down shirt as he composed a song.

I'd like to think that I was his Muse. He titled it "Sing Child, Dance Child."

Is it possible to hear the voice of God in all acts of creation?

"Sing child, dance child. Set yourself free"

December 20, 2015

Quakerlandia, as I've started referring to it, is quite a place. It's hard to believe that this is my life. I never would have imagined it.

My room in the community farmhouse is beautiful. There is a full-size bed and two windows that look out upon rolling hills, a roll-top desk, and a sweet loft that I can reach by ladder.

I bet you'd get along well with Jens. He likes to work with his hands and spends his morning tending sheep—a dream I know you have, but you keep on tending numbers on spreadsheets.

Paul is quite a character. He and his wife are always bickering. But I know deep down they truly love each other.

Then there is the young Jewish couple. They have a son and another baby is on the way. I am floored to learn that they too used to live on 116th Street.

All those years living practically next door to each other, and of all the places, we meet here.

They say I have *ruach*. It's Hebrew for wind or breath of God. I feel like that's just another way of saying I've got soul.

Ellen, one of the founding members of the community, is dying, preparing to shed the final skin.

I'm awkward around her. I don't want to be reminded that I actually do know how the story ends.

Six feet underground. That should be no surprise. Mortality is a reality of life.

Claire, the other woman who lives in the farmhouse with me, is sweet, spunky, and strong like an ox.

The other night like a bunch of teenagers we drank whiskey in the loft of her bedroom.

We tried to make a rap about the difference between the Shakers and the Quakers.

It didn't turn out so well, but we had fun.

In the mornings, I play my flute in the woods. The community has taken to calling me the Forest Elf. But I sense I've come to meet the Forest Queen.

January 9, 2016

Though still bound legally, we decide to cut the spiritual cord, in a ceremony in that sacred spiral that you so diligently keep mowed.

> *I promise to continually support, prod, and nurture your unfolding.*

We take hold of a red ribbon. The one we tied around our heads in a sweat lodge in Tulum.

And you didn't think we'd find one off the beaten path.

You should have known that when you leave it up to me I make our dreams reality.

Sweating our prayers with Mayan elders and loud Italians, I couldn't think of a better way to be born into marriage.

Except for the fact that you lost your wedding band at the site of an ancient Mayan temple that they claim is a vortex.

You dove into the waters of the mangrove canal, showed me your hand, and the ring was gone.

Only three days after having said "I do."

And now as I burn this ribbon I see that it's true, that love requires me to choose my own soul over you.

> *I promise to relish in your joys and be a shoulder for you to cry on in your sorrow . . .*

So much pain in letting this here ribbon go. I plead, "Help me! I can't do it."

If there is so much love, why let go?

THE WEST

You guide my hand in placing it into the fire; our combined breaths help sustain the flame incinerating a marriage that didn't leave us enough room to breathe.

I weep in your arms, looking at the ash of that ribbon and I'm grateful it isn't you. Though this marriage is dead, you are warm in my arms.

But one day we will be dust too.

You'd think knowing this we'd hold onto each other more tightly, but love and life seems to be a journey of letting go.

As the flame burns out, I see clearly through these tears that there is a light that lives in you and me that is stronger than all of our darkness and all of our fears.

The reason to let go is simple. We must die a thousand deaths to truly live in this lifetime.

February 14, 2016

Teachers at school are making Valentines for all the children. I tell them I find the holiday cheesy.

My love isn't dictated by the demands of Hallmark, plus I'm not the crafty type.

I've got no Valentine, just a rotting marriage that lingers on because for some reason neither of us has the guts to file for an actual divorce.

The math teacher, Jake, gives me those schoolgirl butterflies. The kind I haven't felt in ages.

I just can't help but be attracted to the measured yet playful way he strives for success.

He is the structure to my chaos. He's even taught me how to listen to music again.

I love how he has a song for every season, and the way he has taught me that every season has a song.

Thinking about him, my heart grows soft.

It makes me wish I never read that St. Francis prayer. Is it really better to love than be loved?

I think of Ceil and Don and the way he'd look at her.

I wonder what it would feel like having my King look at me as if I were his Queen.

I don't want to be like the Italian Renaissance poet Gaspara Stampa with her soaring objectless love.

The kind of love I have in my heart is meant to land.

I begrudgingly admit to myself that I'm being bitter about the holiday and decide to visit the dollar store.

The rest of my night I spend making Valentines alone in front of a wood burning stove.

I cut out paper hearts, curl ribbons with a scissor, and attach them to glitter-laden pencils, one at a time.

I'm actually surprisingly content. I wonder if this is my version of stacking logs. I take the time to write each child an individual note.

I begin to imagine the room filled with paper hearts with all the people whose lives have crossed my path.

Soon enough the room begins to fill and I'm swimming in a vast sea of paper hearts.

There goes Hamdan, the first boy I taught English to. Ooh and then of course, that tea man in Marrakesh.

And that woman whose magnificent smile caught my eye, as I danced the rumba in a square in Old Havana.

Surely there is more to love than romance. I think life was better when we were children, when love was simply love.

March 11, 2016

The librarian placed a copy of an illustration that I asked her to print for me on my desk.

A former student of mine reached out to me close to when I was completing my first round in the Wheel and I asked if she could draw me a picture based on the poem Julie wrote for me:

Blue Winged Star Dancer

She drew a six-armed woman made of fire and ice.

A full moon behind her head as she rises from the darkness.

Two hands cover her throat . . .

I wonder if there is a Goddess who lives inside of me?

Little Katie enters my room to come and read with me. I show her the image and ask her what she sees.

"What do you mean?" she says.

"Just write. Say whatever you feel. What does the picture mean to you?"

I give her some Post-it Notes and sit quietly at her side.

I can see that wild, fearless girl wisdom start to arise.

Katie writes:

"If you don't say it out loud you are missing the meaning of life."

And then another:

"If you expand you are giving the world more room to breathe."

THE WEST

And then another:

 "My life is your life, so we can expand together."

I hold the Post-its in my hand and I look at her and I feel as if I am in the presence of God.

Her eyes are wide.

 I ask her what she feels.

She tells me: "Love."

March 12, 2016

Our ESL department is hosting a family literacy night in the primary school.

We are reading wordless picture books and showing families how they don't need to even be able to read in English to support their child's literacy.

I sit in a small group and facilitate a conversation, but when I go to the bathroom I suddenly just feel this deep sense of dis-ease.

I meander my way into one of the primary school classrooms and I get this overwhelming feeling that I've been there before.

I take notice of a poster that says "Teach Peace"

I look at it. My throat tightens.

How am I supposed to teach something that I have yet to truly feel?

An unexpected guest comes knocking at the door of my mind.

"Who is there?"

Fear.

I don't want to let him in. Not here, not at school, but he is persistent and knocks down the door.

You are scheduled to be flying back from Japan tonight and I can't get it out of my head that your plane is going to crash.

I go back and forth in my mind if what I am feeling is paranoia or a true premonition.

How can one even tell the difference?

I frantically text you, and tell you that I don't want you to get on that plane.

But you refuse to give into my fear.

My phone of course dies, I have no charger, and I begin to cry.

The mothers from my ESL class at church come to see if I am alright. "Maestra, que pasa?"

I excuse myself, tell the department head that I'm not feeling so well.

Gloria follows me outside to my car and looks at me with utter tenderness.

She reminds me that I'm still grieving.

"Todo sera bien, Maestra. Tranquila. Respira."

March 16, 2016

On the card table Claire has dumped out a puzzle and placed a sign on it that says, "Unpuzzle your Mind."

It's the purest reflection of my inner world that I could ever come across. I feel like a bunch of scattered puzzle pieces.

I'm sure to the rest of the world, I appear quite strange, maybe even crazy.

But this place I call reality feels like nothing but a mirage, it's as if the curtain at any moment is about to be lifted.

My bedroom is strewn with clothes and it reminds me of that time my mother and I had that fight when she dumped my bag of giveaways on the floor.

I ended up stepping on a sewing needle and punctured my foot. She then held me in her arms and we both cried.

Normally I am much more ordered than this, but I have given in to the part of me that tells me there is order in this mess.

I want to be in "control" but I can't. I'm falling apart, and maybe that is actually okay?

I go to my altar to pray.

I stare at a painting of Noah's Ark with a rainbow and White Unicorn standing on a rock.

It says, "We must Believe in Rainbows"

And I hope that belief is enough.

I drive to school feeling like raw spirit dressed up in human form.

THE WEST

The mist lays low on Red Rock Road. I pause at a lonely intersection and I see a fox on the hill.

Never saw one this close in my life. I stop the car and stare directly in his eyes.

He doesn't move, nor flinch. Tells me of a future that feels all too big.

"Who, me?" I say.

"Yes, you."

The fox says he's come to teach me to see the invisible amidst the visible, and magic among the meek.

Later at school, in the reading bin I catch a glimpse of a book called *Fox's Dream*.

It calls out to me. I thumb through it as the children work on math problems.

I read the description.

Wandering through a winter forest, a lonely fox has an enchanting vision and then finds the companionship for which he has been longing.

I wonder if I am his vixen and we've stumbled into each other's visions.

As a little girl I wrote a poem about a fox that my mother saved. It simply read:

> *A lonely fox springs into the world, learning life alone.*

I turn around and Connor has a t-shirt that says, "One day they'll make a movie of my life," and I wonder if the script has already been written.

It's hard to be at work around so many people.

I feel safe only in front of the nonjudgmental eyes of my students. I see a part of myself in each of them.

Ruthie walks by with her snorting laughter and I'm reminded of the way I used to laugh like that.

My short hair and spunky and rebellious ways.

How did I lose my laugh? Where did that little rebel girl go?

That girl who, when her second-grade classmate told her that a woman would never be president, held an impromptu rally in the school yard and got all the kids to chant "Dina for President!"

……..Where did she go?

That girl who, when she caught a glimpse of Tank Man during the Tiananmen Square Massacre, wept the entire night, then walked into her principal's office the next morning to demand the children stage a walk-out.

………Where did she go?

Did she depart from me that day she stood in front of her elementary school's morning program and words failed to express the wisdom of her heart, and she walked away feeling misunderstood and utterly ashamed?

Did she depart from me that day after the Rodney King beating when she watched Los Angeles go up in flames and grabbed her mother's hand, crying, "Why, Mommy, why?"

I feel this divine child alive inside of me. And all she wants is to return to a wonderland of lost innocence, and truly trust that all is well.

THE WEST

When I get to school I go to Jake's room. It's a bit awkward.

I just confessed to him the other day that I have feelings for him, and he doesn't feel the same.

But I need him right now like I've never needed him before.
He appears to shudder at the sight of me.

I'm a mess, I know.
My hair disheveled, all boundaries of my being broken.

My need for him must feel like he is being engulfed.
I put my hands up. I ask how much space he needs.
Five steps back? Ten steps back? More?

"I don't need you to understand me," I plead. "I need you to just be you!"

He seems to relax a bit.
I crave his solid boundaries and lighthearted humor.

The world is exuding too much meaning; I am drowning in metaphor.

I need him to tell me that a cracker is just a cracker, that a desk is just a desk, and a chair is just a chair.

Please tell me that this world of so much meaning is also meaningless.

He is afraid, but he stays. I ask, "What do I do?"

"I don't know."

"Yes, you do."

I know a deep wisdom resides in him. I see it in that sparkle in his eyes.

I feel it when he clearly says, "Yes" and though it hurts, wisdom is palpable even in his "No."

He closes his eyes and speaks from his intuitive and kind heart.

He tells me to write a letter, say what needs to be said, put it in an envelope, and fill it with natural elements.

As I leave his room, I take note of his "Binder of Shame."

A few months ago I laughed at it.

It's where all the students write their excuse for not doing their homework, but when I look at it in the state I'm in, it makes me sick.

My sensitivity is so that I can feel the way in which guilt and shame slowly seep into our being, making us smaller versions of ourselves.

"Jacob, you need to get rid of this," I demand.

He firmly stands his ground, "No, I don't."

This is us wrestling.

March 20, 2016

I can't stop the connections and the meaning-making.

Claire is concerned.

My mind has become a splattering of Post-it Notes strewn all over my bedroom wall.

It's like a scene from *A Beautiful Mind*.

Jake texts and sends me a cute bitmoji that urges me to rest.

It's good to know he cares.

There is one Post-it Note that I hang directly above my bed.

It says, "Eat, sleep, dance, shit, attend to basics."

A reminder that I live in both a spiritual and material world.

Claire sends Dan, the social worker in our community, to check on me. He climbs up the ladder to my loft and joins me in my sacred space.

"Do you think you might want to go to the hospital?" he asks.

I can tell he says that out of care, but I would not dare. I know I seem crazy, but I have to guard my psychic space.

I saw my father give in to fear, and he ended up with a diagnosis when all he needed was a witness.

"No! This is between me and God. Just give me a few days"

He obliges, covers me with blankets, and walks down the ladder.

I lay there huddled in a fetal position feeling an overwhelming sense of oppression, the walls of my mind, collapsing in upon me.

I'm grasping at any thought that will lead me out of this maze. Any thought that will help me make sense of this overwhelming pain.

"Why God? I plead"

I suddenly recall that my grandmother on my father's side whose name I bear.

Nonna Dina. A Pennsylvania woman whose cabin in the woods always smelled of mold.

A cold yet hardworking woman whom my grandfather Victor loved. On their 60th anniversary you could still see they had a sparkle in their eyes.

The next thought that enters my mind is that her birthday is shared by Hitler.

A conversation ensues between me and some voice. Maybe it's God? Maybe a higher self? Or Maybe I am just crazy.

"Go with it. The voice says. What does that mean to you?"

"I don't know. From the pain I feel it's as if I were Hitler in a past life?"

"Perhaps"

I try to shrug that idea off as it if it were crazy and yet this voice in me tells me to stay with that thought without any judgement.

I comply and I contemplate the possibility of that being true and as I do I feel as if I'm being pounded by waves of guilt and regret.

This voice presses, "Let's just suppose you were Hitler in a past life, how would that change things now?"

The mere thought is unbearable. How can one even begin to reconcile such hate?

Yet the voice persists, "If you were Hitler in a past life, would you forgive yourself now? Yes or no?"

I begin to think that Dan was right. Maybe I do need to go to the hospital.

But the voice urges me to stay, urges me to trust that these questions are leading me somewhere.

"So, you are willing to waste this precious life of yours in regret because of a past that you couldn't control?"

My soul is being pressed.

"No," I whisper. "So what do I do?"

"Can you forgive?"

This is fucking crazy. Who am I even talking to?

The voice persists. "Would you forgive?"

"I don't know. Did God forgive Hitler? Is there really some eternal hell that separates the "good" from the "bad"?

"Does it matter? I'm asking you if you would forgive?"

Pressed between what my mother likes to refer to as a rock and a hard place, I finally give in.

"Yes…..I forgive. I want to live!" I cry. "I am worthy of this life"

The waves of regret transform into soft lapping waves of inconceivable mercy that lull me to sleep.

March 21, 2016

I text Jake and tell him I'm not coming to school.

I slowly walk downstairs to the kitchen. I pour myself a glass of water and hear Jens in the laundry room.

I walk over to say hello and I fall into his arms and cry.

He says to go and connect with the Earth.

I walk out to my rock and begin to play my flute.

I am thankful for the simplicity of my reverberating breath.

There is a garbage can on the right side of the field and as I stare at it something in my soul tells me it needs to be purged.

I think about Jake's advice to just write. To let out all that needs to be said.

My pen begins to bleed in reclamation of my intuitive Self . . .

. . . All of HER . . .

Her heart,
the drum

Her breath,
the wind that scatters tribal seeds of truth

Her feet,
the paws of a tiger calm and precise
one step at a time,
ready to pounce
when the moment is right

….ALL of HER……

the virgin and the prostitute
the witch and the Saint

….ALL of HER

I grasp onto the rock, lay down my head,
and fall in and out of a hazy dream.

When I finally find the strength, I walk back to the community farmhouse

On the kitchen counter is a coloring page of Moses and the burning bush.

I hold it in my hands and I realize, that Heaven truly does exist here on Earth.

April 12, 2016

I sign Sheepfold Farm over to you today. It is easier this way. No fight. What's yours is yours, and what's mine is mine.

I'm saddened we didn't fill that barn with more song, and the community that I developed in your absence didn't have an opportunity to dance in the hay.

It's hard to imagine that three years ago in this very office we were happily our signing our closing documents, about to eat our celebratory chocolate cake.

The secretary asks for my ID.

I crack a joke. Humor fills in grooves carved by life's sorrows.

It's surreal, this world of legalities. Ink traverses paper. The formation of letters binds us, and breaks us apart.

I go to the Victory Chapel next door to pray. It is empty. I like it this way.

The Virgin of Guadalupe is at my side and our Lady Queen of Victory, with her crown above me, is shining bright.

Behind her is a wall with the names inscribed of the young and the brave who—for the red, white, and blue—sacrificed their flesh and blood.

I'm perplexed.

I thought the cross had already been carried. If Victory has been won, then why do I weep?

As my hand caresses these names, I recall our wedding day in a green oasis in the midst of a desert valley 44.4 kilometers away from where Miguel de Hidalgo made his famous Grito de Dolores.

The flame above the statue of St. Jude's head is now ablaze in my heart and I hear the sound of Spanish guitars playing *Romanza de Amor*.

I taste the sweet and bitter wine we drank during the Celtic Loving Cup ceremony.

I recall Miranda's words when she said: "Those who drink from the Loving Cup, with an open heart and willing spirit, invite the full range of challenges and experiences into their being."

Had I known what that would have brought, I think I would have been a bit more hesitant about taking a sip.

On my knees a movie of our wedding day plays before me.

Ardie reads from Kahlil Gibran's *The Prophet*. We say "I do" and kiss.

I hear the twelve-piece mariachi band. I see us leading our guests up and around the hacienda, waving our animal maracas.

We are greeted by a disgruntled tequila-laden burro and twelve-foot-tall papier-mâché mojigangas.

There is a bride, a groom, and a sexy lady in a red dress. My friend Nick face-plants into her voluptuous breasts.

With the fire ablaze in my heart I see that her inclusion in our wedding was not a mere accident.

I didn't recall inviting another woman to partake in our marriage.

I ponder if she was merely a prop on the stage of life foreshadowing affairs to come.

But no, she was me, that Lady in Red.

The lustful, dark, attention seeking, never satisfied woman with an unquenchable thirst brought to life in front of my very own eyes.

And seven years later, I see why *the oak tree and the cypress grow not in each other's shadow.*

You only ever tried to love me in the way that you knew how.

I leave the Victory Chapel and you pull up.

It's your turn to move ink across paper; another step closer to breaking this covenant.

We embrace.

Oh Lady in Red, saved by grace, I hear the Warrior's cry!

The North—
Taking Hold of the Sacred Thread

*There's a thread you follow. It goes among
things that change. But it doesn't change.
People wonder about what you are pursuing.
You have to explain about the thread.
But it is hard for others to see.
While you hold it you can't get lost.
Tragedies happen; people get hurt
or die; and you suffer and get old.
Nothing you do can stop time's unfolding.
You don't ever let go of the thread.*

~ William Stafford ~

May 18, 2016

A student with pink tips at the end of her hair leans against the wall.

I ask, "On a scale of 1 to 10 how is your day?"

She smirks.

I'm taken by her shirt. It is of a wolf, half white and half black.

Its eyes penetrate me and I'm reminded of that Cherokee legend of the two wolves.

"So, what does this image mean to you?" I ask.

She looks at her shirt, interest piqued. "I've never thought about it."

I tell her to go home and write about it. I warn her not to look it up—to trust her own interpretation instead.

She meets me the next morning and kneels down and takes pages of loose-leaf paper from her folder.

She hands me her work, proud as can be. "I've never written something like this before."

I begin to read . . .

"The she wolf lifted its head to the star-filled sky. Taking in the cool crisp air she let out a howl . . . Then the voices came. They had been with her since she was a pup. She knew them as Nyx and Lux. . . . The two start fighting with one another whenever she decides to do something, making her second-guess herself. She listened to them both and they quieted down. She needed both Lux and Nyx, they made her who she was even if they disagreed with each other. They were part of her, they shaped who she is, and she was Astra-Star Dancer."

June 8, 2016

I ran into Jake's classroom a few weeks ago inspired by a video of a town in Norway that installed a sign that encourages the people to do a Monty Python silly walk as they cross the street.

"We've got to do the same!" I exclaimed. "An Ichabod Crane Silly Walking Day!"

Jake and I recruited other teachers in the planning process and strategized together as if we were in the War Room.

I can't even begin to explain how refreshing it feels to take silliness in such a serious way. It is medicine for my heart and Soul.

I walk into the fourth-grade classrooms to announce that they have a big role to play if they want Silly Walking Day to be a success.

Eric shoots his arm in the air. "Yea guys, we have to teach the eighth-graders how to be kids again."

In between classes the hallways are filled with silly walkers. Even some teachers who I never thought would crack a smile are letting go.

It's funny how afraid we are to be "silly."

I decided last week to look up the etymology of *silly*. It actually means "happy, fortuitous, and prosperous."

But somewhere along the line the meaning moved from "happy" to "blessed" to "feeble in mind," to "lacking in reason," and to "foolish."

Funny the things we call foolish.

In a world that is constantly being duped by its "leaders" spouting fear and hate, I think I'd rather be the fool.

June 24, 2016

I'm sitting on the back porch of the farmhouse and my inner tyrant won't leave me alone.

Demanding me to Do, Do, Do!

Teaching isn't enough….The tyrant tells me I must do more….

"The world is falling apart," it screams. "What are you going to DO about it?"

I'm tired of feeling like it's my sacred duty to save the world.

Every time I do I come face to face with my own fragility. It is a feat enough to save myself.

Why is nothing ever enough?

Why isn't it enough to simply take notice of the stripes on this chipmunk's back?

Why isn't it enough for me to merely sit here and witness the way in which he stuffs his cheeks full?

……..Why must I do, do, do?

……..Why does this inner tyrant push me so much?

You know what I want to do?

I want to run through the woods and find the loneliest tree, wrap my arms around her and say:

"I LOVE YOU. YOU ARE SEEN!"

Do not all of God's creatures deserve a witness?

July 9, 2016

My best friend's daughter and I are taking a road trip to Washington D.C. for a march called Save Our Schools.

With the windows down, we blast the soundtrack to "Hamilton."

My friend's daughter is a brilliant girl, perhaps a bit spoiled, but she's got fire alright.

Halfway through our trip my car breaks down. The tow truck guy tells me that it's the timing belt.

I call you in a panic. I think it is some sign to go back. You tell me, it does not mean that I am supposed to go back. You tell me that it simply means that the timing belt is broken.

You save the day with clear, crisp, unemotional logic. You arrange a rental for us, and remind me that everything is okay and that signs are what we make them.

I'm starting to see that I have a propensity to make meaning, when there is no meaning to be made.

I used to think that was you just being cold. I'm recalling now why I fell in love with you.

We hang up and I sit on the curb and burst into tears.

"Maybe we are making a mistake." My friend's daughter looks at me, shaking her head.

"Oh Dina! It means you are friends. My mom and dad are the same. They aren't together but they still help one another out."

Nothing like a thirteen-year-old to set you straight.

We arrive at the National Mall just in time to hear a young black boy give a tearful speech.

He expresses his fears of becoming another hashtag. He then gives a rousing call to fight for justice for all.

He reminds me of the little girl I used to be who knew how to take a stand for the things in which she believed.

Reverend Barber speaks next and though the mall is far from full, I feel like I am standing in the nascent stages of an earthshaking movement.

His booming voice makes the hair on my arms stand tall.

"Our greatest religious traditions," he says, "tell us that children are gifts and that children must be welcomed and cared for if a nation is going to be great and if a nation is going to honor God. But when you undermine the dreams of the children, you undermine the dreams of a nation."

He speaks of making the beloved community a reality and we chant, "Forward together and not one step back."

July 26, 2016

I'm in an antique store in San Salvador, Brazil. It's the first time I'm travelling internationally on my own again.

I've just arrived from Sao Paulo, a place where my ancestors spent ten years before boarding a ship to New York.

Before my trip, I had been reading my great-aunt Zizi Tessie's handwritten manuscript of my great-grandparents' history entitled "The Players."

In it she described the trials, tribulations, and joys of a young Sicilian couple as they uprooted their family and set out to create a new life for themselves in Brazil.

She didn't finish it.... but at least I know now where all that *saudade* of my soul comes from.

…..I grab a book off the shelf by Richard Bach. It's called *A Ponte Para o Sempre*.

"A Bridge Across Forever."

I read the opening lines.

Pensamos as vezes que não restou um só dragão. Nao ha mais qualquer bravo cavaleiro, nem uma única princesa a planar por florestas secretas, encantando cervos o borboletas com seu sorriso.

Seu sorriso . . .

"Her Smile."

My first love wrote a story about my smile for his AP English class.

He read it to me one night on the phone and my heart nearly melted.

There is nothing quite like young love.

We used to fall asleep talking to each other on the phone. I'd wake up in the middle of the night hearing him pressing the buttons to wake me.

When he'd leave my house, we had this ritual where he'd flicker his lights all the way until his car was out of sight.

I leave the store and begin to wander my way through barrio San Antonio and it feels as if I am meandering my way through my own love story.

When it begins to rain I duck into the Igreja Da Ordem do Carmo and walk over to the wooden carving of a reclining Jesus kept in a glass case. Carved by Francisco Xavier das Chagas, O Cabra, a former slave of the order that worked there.

I look closer and I see the blood of Christ is made out of rubies.

Jesus's blood made in rubies by a former slave.

I don't know whether I should scream, cry, or laugh.

Perhaps all three.

And the world said Madonna was a whore for using her art to bring us to our knees.

The hypocrites go on repeating history, but Madonna had it right all along.

Life is a mystery,
everyone must stand alone;
I hear you call my name
and it feels like home.

September 28, 2016

It's 7:00 a.m. before the start of school and a small group of us are gathered for an event called See You at the Pole. It's a day to promote Christian prayer.

My principal is here, another teacher, a few students from my Spanish class, and their parents. The father of one of my students is a pastor of one of the local churches that I've been warned is one of those "crazy evangelical types."

It's strange to be doing things like this. If you told me a few years ago I'd be standing here at this pole, I would never have believed it.

I would have said that is far too "God and Country" for me.

But I have to admit, I kind of like it.

It's nice to gather, bow my head with my students and colleagues, and take a moment to acknowledge that perhaps there is something greater at hand than running up the damn ladder of achievement, while we pretend to live in a society that actually cares to leave no child behind.

Everyone begins to share their prayers aloud, but my mouth is sealed shut. Even if I wished to speak, Spirit wouldn't have it.

All this Dear-Lord-Father stuff feels strange to me. I am more comfortable saying God, Creator, Mother Earth and Father Sky.

If it were up to me this would be just a day of prayer and not necessarily "Christian" prayer.

But I listen for truth and wisdom in whatever name it's wrapped up in.

The pastor begins to speak. He talks about the name of our school, and how Ichabod isn't just the name of a quirky schoolteacher from Washington Irving's *The Legend of Sleepy Hollow*.

He says it's from the Bible. Its meaning being that the "glory of God has departed."

Quite a namesake for a school.

He then prays over the school and all of the children, teachers and staff it houses.

He asks that each of us are able to develop the talents and gifts that the Lord has bestowed upon us.

He prays for each person to be able to meet his/her highest God-given potential.

I find an unexpected softness in my heart as he speaks these words.

He doesn't seem like a "crazy evangelical" to me. His words sound like a prayer that anyone with a decent heart would say.

He continues praying that as each of us meet our highest God-given potential that the glory of God will be returned.

I begin to feel that latent creative potential in me stir. I think it's what I've been running from my whole entire life.

Why is it that I can pull the glimmer of potential I see in others out with an encouraging word, but when it comes to my own I become stricken with fear and doubt.

I wonder if there are gifts that God has given me that I have yet to even discover.

This big bright personality of mine is quite the guise; could it be that my soul is just shy?

October 14, 2016

My principal told me I should take the rest of the day and go home and rest.

I got dizzy after class and another teacher grabbed me and brought me to the nurse.

I'm having trouble maintaining the mask. I literally can't tell the difference between my personal pain and the world's pain.

I'm afraid I have failed at containing my humanity.

I am told students are not supposed to see their teacher cry.

…..Why?

They don't judge my sensitivity. In fact, they seem to rise as my unarmored weaknesses call forth their strengths.

The nurse gives me a Capri Sun and crackers as she rubs my back and tells me it's okay to cry.

….The blood and the bread.

This is the communion of kindness.

With unexpected time on my hands, I decide to drop by the farm. It's your house now. I must remind myself it is no longer mine.

But I can still love the land that held me so. Though the deed no longer bears my name, my tears have watered her soils.

It is the land where I learned to listen to the wisdom of the rustling leaves and to feel the Earth's heartbeat underneath my own feet.

It's the land where I discovered that trees are beings and they like it when I sing them sweet melodies.

It's the land where I learned to stroke the small of my back, to put myself to sleep, and to sing the fear away.

…When I arrive, I walk into the middle of our lawn and I fall to my knees.

I'm juxtaposed between the dying elm, and the ash with its broken branch. The strong and tall oak sits behind my back.

Suddenly, I'm lifted to my feet.

I go to the barn and grab the front-door key. I don't care about your privacy.

I head straight to our bedroom and walk into our old closet. I see another woman's clothes where mine used to be. She wears a size XS and has pretty panties.

I stare hoping for this reality to burn through the last illusions of hope and then I let myself out.

I am tired of this psychotic belief that the reconciliation of this world rests upon the reconciliation of our marriage.

Could it be that God just actually wants me to be fucking happy?

I walk directly to the oak tree and wrap my arms around her. I wonder if she remembers what it was like to be an acorn buried in the deep dark Earth.

When she began to sprout did she try to go back to the place she knew as home, or did she plow straight toward an open sky and never look behind?

I want to give up, but I must be strong.

THE NORTH

For one day, a little girl afraid of growing up will wrap her arms around the trunk of my body and know, that she too is like the oak.

October 28, 2016

Gloria invited me to a Mexican cooking class she is giving in the basement of the church.

I like to watch the community coming together in this way. Language differences cease to exist with the smell of chilies filling the air.

As the adults watch Gloria do her magic, the children are spinning around the poles in utter delight.

They remind me of the Sufis. Little whirling dervishes that don't need a course in how to be spiritual. They just are.

I look up and stare at a painting of Jesus Christ before me. Below him is a sticker of a ladybug.

I recall that Palm Sunday at that church in Woodstock when I saw one climbing out of the furnace vent.

I didn't think much of it at first, but when I saw another one an hour later perched on the fingertip of a wide-eyed little girl, it made smirk.

Could it be that we are surrounded by everyday miracles just begging us to take notice?

I wonder if this is this what it means to become winged in word and deed.

…."Have you gone to the opening at the Jack Shainman Gallery at The School?" a woman asks.

"No," I say. "Should I go?"

"It's really fabulous, you still have thirty minutes till it closes."

THE NORTH

I won't be able to eat Gloria's delicious food, but I feel a tug that I can't control.

When I arrive at the gallery, I see a rifle covered in honeycomb and I dream of a day when sweet loving tenderness defeats the wickedness of man.

I walk up the stairs and I stare at a work of art by El Anatsui, a Ghanaian sculptor known for his iconic bottle-top installations.

A similar piece hung in the foyer of our condo at the Kalahari in Harlem. When I look closer the title of the piece is called "Ascension."

My heart begins to pound. Is this what it means to ascend with two feet on the ground?

I return to the church, where they have saved me a few tacos. Everyone is cleaning up.

I offer my new friend Diego a ride home and we blast R. Kelly's "I Believe I Can Fly" and I remember that this is what it means to be alive.

I drive home to Quakerland and when I arrive Claire tells me that Ellen has finally let go.

I hate to admit it, but often I wondered what was taking her so long.

Pretty awful thought to have. I can't even fully let go of a marriage and yet I wonder why she hesitated in letting go of her body.

Her death has been meticulously planned. Jens crafted a coffin waiting for this day.

I'm sure people would call me crazy, but if I ran a school I think I'd have the students build their own coffins.

Why in this culture are we so afraid of death?

Why do we pretend that we're above being mortal when it is the inevitability of death that gives so much flavor to life?

We light the driveway in candles.

I play my flute as they walk her body down the gravel path.

The hearse comes and drives her away, and we all return to our rooms and go our separate ways.

October 31, 2016

Tonight the community is holding a sacred fire for Ellen. Someone has put wings on the sheep-crossing sign.

We tell stories around the fire. We cry. We laugh. We are remembering what it means to be human, to be born, to live, and to die.

I stare at the fire, remembering when I didn't trust its ability to hold my pain. Now I know its power to burn illusion away.

As we sit I recall the animated film I showed my class earlier in the day about Dia de Los Muertos.

In the film, a little girl visits her mother's grave and is whisked down into the land of the dead by a magic blue flower. The skeletons run her around, one even takes off an arm and they play piñata.

The little girl begins to smile. The skeleton in the blue skirt then transforms into her mother and they stare into each other's eyes as if there was no such thing as a good-bye.

The little girl leaves the land of the dead with that magic blue flower skipping into life.

My student Josh looks up at me with wide-eyed amazement.

"Ms., I thought Heaven was up, not down!" He then gestures that his mind was just blown and shouts, "It's a paradox!"

I laugh. Kids are so much smarter than adults.

Later in the afternoon, I show the film to my student whose mother died.

She hugs me and smiles. I don't know how she can be so strong.

I can't even begin to imagine life without my mother.

I think about the moment my mom and I recently shared when we were watching *Jane the Virgin.*

There was this scene where Jane's mother Xiomara sang "Dream a Little Dream."

I looked into her eyes, and grasped her aging hand, in a state of whatever the word is when awe meets grief.

She and I loved that song.

We heard it in that Corey Feldman movie where an accident puts the consciousness of an elderly dream researcher into the body of a bratty teenager.

Perhaps that is what God is doing to me….

I wonder if this is what it means when Nina Simone sings that the bible says, "Be transformed by the renewing of your mind"

As we watched that scene, I saw the pain of my mother's unfulfilled dreams of becoming a singer.

We looked into each other's eyes as if time didn't exist; the joy and pain of the mother-daughter relationship encapsulated in one brief moment of unarmed mutual recognition.

I wonder if she knows just how much I yearn to sing the songs that are buried deep in my soul.

Watching that TV show is like watching our lives.

Jane, Xiomara, and Alba,
Dina, Mimi, and Anna . . .

THE NORTH

How nice it would be to sit with my mother and my Nonna again and watch the sand pass through the hourglass of our favorite soap opera, "Days of Our Lives."

…..An ash from the sacred fire falls on my shoulder, and I'm lifted out of the tapestry of memory.

Existence is so fragile . . .

Stars shining bright above you . . .
Night breezes seem to whisper "I love you."
Birds singing in the sycamore trees,
dream a little dream of me . . .

November 2, 2016

Claire must have heard me crying last night.

I woke up to a poem stuck on the mirror with a Post-it that said, "Love you, Dolores."

That's the name Claire calls me when I do all the things that irk her, like leaving dishes in the sink …

And those moments when I get so wrapped up with what's going on inside of me that I forget there is an actual world with people in it who have different needs and wants than my own. The poem reads:

> *Take courage friends.*
> *The way is often hard, the path is never clear,*
> *and the stakes are very high.*
> *Take courage.*
> *For deep down, there is another truth:*
> *You are not alone.*

I forget sometimes that I'm not the first to seek God in this way and I won't be the last.

I message the pastor of the local Lutheran church looking for some words of wisdom.

He is the first trans pastor I have ever met in my life.

I ask him what one is supposed to do when God is driving you mad.

He tells me to go scream in the woods for at least one hour a day.

He seems to think this overwhelming passion I'm feeling is driving me somewhere.

THE NORTH

…..But where?

He tells me that God is kind of like a cat, always pestering and demanding attention.

Tells me I might as well give in.

I joke and tell him that God sounds kind of like me.

November 6, 2016

Jake is out knocking on doors getting out the vote as I sit at my desk trying to write the demons away.

After hours of being glued to my seat, I go to the cafe and see my friend Marie Claude.

She tells me that there is an Our Lady of Lourdes shrine not too far away in New Lebanon.

I decide to go.

The Blessed Mother stands before me.

I take notice of the prayers laid down at her feet.

I feel less alone seeing that others too have fallen to their knees not knowing where life was leading.

I take my prayer purse from my bag and lay out all of my cards on the stones.

Saint Anthony, Saint Kateri, Saint Therese, and some Pokémon cards some children gave me at school.

Is there even a difference between the two, or does love shine through all things?

From my purse I take a small glass jar filled with colored bits of wood.

I picked it up in a Bolivian witch market a month before I met my Chilean love.

Thinking of the ten years I spent trapped in romantic illusion, it appears that there is a great difference between love that bewitches and love that saves.

I lay the little love potion at her feet as an offering to the healing of our world.

To the Blessed Mother I pray:

"Help me to release my desire to wrap a man's love around me as if my own beating heart weren't enough. I give unto you all the love that I seek."

November 8, 2016

It's a misty morning and it's got me wondering if the whole planet is in a fog.

I can't see the hills on the other side of the Hudson. From the river to the sky I see several shades of grey.

It is hard to believe that I woke up to the news that Donald Trump is now our president.

Yet, for some strange reason after hearing the news I found myself singing in the shower:

I can see clearly now the rain is gone, I can see all obstacles in my way . . .

I remember singing that song when Obama got elected. We were coming home drunk from a friend's election party.

I sat on the subway filled with hope and wanted to hear that song and celebrate.

The guy sitting next to me happened to have it. He shared his earbud with me and we sang aloud.

A few others joined in, but in my mind the whole subway would break out into song and dance.

Gone are the dark clouds that had me down,
It's gonna be a bright, bright, bright, sunshiny day

You ignored me.

Stood there staring at your Blackberry, pretending I didn't exist.

I've got to admit, it seems the starkness of reality stripped of hope is actually more hopeful than illusion.

THE NORTH

I stare at the river, which flows both ways, and notice that she is absolutely still.

She tells me to mimic her wise ways.

I listen as she speaks: *Lean into the unknown; trust that the mist will rise and you will come to see the sun on the other side.*

When I get to school, I walk into Jake's classroom and he is sullen.

My joy is disruptive to his dismay, and he tells me to go away.

November 13, 2016

I am walking through the Chatham grocery store and a Hallmark card catches my eye.

It says: *Granddaughter, nobody can give to the world what you have to give. Nobody can smile your smile, laugh your laugh, shine your light, be wonderful in the way that is so uniquely you. Could there be any better reason to celebrate?*

I buy the card. I take it home and sit at my roll-top desk.

I stare at the painting of my childhood home at 29 Washington Avenue and remember those good old days when we would howl at the moon from our back porch singing "That's Amore."

I think about that magical tower where my Nonna and her sister Tess sowed their prayers.

She tells me to write and just let go of the need to control. The truth is that I no longer care if this is my imagination or if it is really Her.

Gioia,

I see you. I stand at your back, just right from center, and I place my hand on your shoulder. Do you feel my touch? You have a beautiful and unique light to share.

You are an angel of God brought here to spread love. Simply follow your desires and God and I will handle the rest in fulfilling each and every one of your dreams. Poco a poco se va lontano.

Trust step by step. Enjoy a glass of scotch and be good to yourself. Set aside some buttered saltine crackers from time to time.

Oh, my little butterfly chaser is learning how to be a dragonfly. Hang in balance and let joy lift your wings.

Nonna

November 26, 2016

Today you are cutting down the old elm. It started as a little yellowing around the crown; we tried to ignore the signs but they couldn't be denied.

We circled around the tree like a bunch of hippies. Held it in our prayers, made offerings.

Soon after you called Bob the Tree Guy. He said, "Dutch elm disease wins every time."

But I was determined that strong prayer could stamp out death.

I remember on closing day, when we'd bought the property, how I'd caught a glimpse of the Janeways saying good-bye.

They stood before the old elm, wrapped in each other's arms. I took a picture of them in my mind's eye.

I recall the doorway leading to the basement and the lines they drew marking their children's height.

I imagined we'd mark the growth of our own child on that same door.

Willy was a tall fellow; his children not too far behind. My parents too had marked my height on the wall.

It was so good to be reminded of home…….
I wish you had memories like mine.

But the day has finally come to accept that death is an equal part of life.

And what started as a yellowing at the crown will give way to purple majesty.

Who knew that the well where the bees had made their hive gave way to the Living Water?

The day you cut down the poison tree will be marked in history.

She is now a stack of logs perfectly arranged and I wonder if your own soul has such perfect order.

The ancestors must have heard us the day we blessed this land, reawakening sacred soils and bringing darkness into light.

I offer my mistakes to the Mother.

May they fertilize and nourish this Earth.

Not having borne a child of my own, I mark the height of my own growth on the ancient doorway of God's gate.

It is now certain; the fire in me is sustained with steady breath.

Thank you, old elm. You have taught me well.

December 17, 2016

My boat has been set adrift and I've grown accustomed to sailing these unknown seas. But now I'm awaiting my anchor, he who will set this Wild Child free.

Who is he?
That keeps me up at night, that guards my tender heart, and keeps me safe. That moves my body in such a way that reminds me I'm made of river tides and ocean waves.

Who is he?
That has depth, who sources his joy from his pain, and yearns to know the gift of a woman's grace, yet doesn't tremble at the intensity of her gaze.

Who is he?
I've got a soundtrack to my afterlife that I've been listening to on repeat, waiting for that moment when we meet and our two hearts both skip a beat.

Who is he?
That is unafraid of being brought to his knees in ecstasy of love that's not dressed in illusion, but love that is raw, naked, and writhing on the floor.

Who is he?
That runs his fingers down my body, giving greetings and thanks to each and every pore.

Who is he?
That awaits the moment I return home to lick the salty remains from the nape of my neck, after dancing all night long to the rhythms of Guaguancó.

Who is he?
That has ascended with two feet on the ground, not enraptured in some romantic dream, but craves a love that is real and profound.

Who is he?

"Have patience my dear," I hear Her say.

"For what you seek is what you find, for you are living now in the meantime. So rejoice in this struggle, as it leads you to the light, for life is sourced from this waiting feeling inside."

December 22, 2016

Joy and pain rub against each other igniting a spark, and the dreamer in me is now on fire.

My mind seeks unity in everything I see. My student shows me his worksheet.

It's entitled "Cells Unite." I smirk. How long until we learn to mimic our sacred nature?

The bottom of the worksheet compares the parts of a cell to a town, and describes the important role each person plays in it.

Oh, how I long to live in a simpler world where I take my worn shoes to the shoemaker who replaces my sole and simultaneously touches it.

Another student later asks me what an integer means. We look it up and write its definition in the margins.

Moments after, another student walks in. She has the words *whole, rational, and integer* taped onto her part-time mermaid t-shirt.

It's almost overwhelming the way the sacred shines through all things.

I see now why I've always had trouble calculating fractions, it's because I know deep down that we are whole and complete.

My problem though exists when we treat people like numbers, leaving society to define so many in the margins.

December 30, 2016

I'm at my friend Todd's place in Brooklyn when I recall the "We Are All One…Year of Mercy" poster, which I've had in the trunk of my car ever since that peace vigil at the Hudson Islamic Center.

I decide that this is the day that my faith is more important than other people's opinions.

I run to Target and buy a Darth Vader mask then make my way to the Ghandi statue in Union Square.

I stand there with my poster and no one really seems to care nor notice.

I suddenly realize I'm "that woman."

There is a Chinese Fire Monkey across from me and I run and give him a hug.

I then shout to the people passing by, "Feel your feelings. The dark ones too. Mercy is the force!"

Several people ignore me. Some smile and I even get a few hugs.

I make friends with a Senegalese man and we sit on a bench and talk. I tell him to go visit his family before it is too late.

Before going home, a little boy and his mother pass me and I surprise him with my Darth Vader mask.

He walks off in a happy skip and I watch him and his mother till they get to the end of the block.

The fiery passion all consuming passion seems to be slowly transforming into calm self-content.

December 31, 2016

I don't care to do anything in particular this New Year's, other than just spend the day with my own thoughts and see where the day leads.

After a little stop in my hometown of Nyack, I make my way back up north to Hudson and stop at St. Mary's.

I am mesmerized by the nativity scene. There are life-size statues of the three kings; Mary; her husband, Joseph; and that baby Jesus radiating his love and light.

As I stare at that baby in the manger, I just get this overwhelming feeling like little baby Christ and little baby Dina are one and the same, and suddenly my imagination is set ablaze.

One of the Three Wise Men reaches his hand out to me and we begin to salsa dance in the middle of this old church.

The animals in the manger come to life and it's a party like I've never experienced before.

My fantasy though is soon interrupted by a black woman in her mid-forties who enters the church.

All the statues return to their places. She walks up to the altar and we both continue to stare in silence.

"Isn't it beautiful?" she asks.

I look at her, nod, and begin to cry. My tears seem to be an invitation for her own catharsis and she immediately comes toward me and falls into my arms.

"I'm tired," she says. "When will He come back?"

"I don't know, probably when we all start acting like Him?"

She then proceeds to confess to me as if I were a priest. Tells me that she isn't the perfect person but is really trying hard to do her best.

"None of us are perfect," I say.

Then I make my own confession.

"Listen, if I have too many drinks all of a sudden I turn into Lusty Lucy and before I know it, I pull a sexy meet-me-in-the-bathroom eyes with the guy I've been flirting with at the bar."

We fall over in a knowing laughter. Doesn't everyone have sexy meet-me-in the-bathroom eyes?

The priest hears us making a racket; comes over and tells us that he is closing up for the night.

I drive her home and we hug good-bye.

I then make my way to Chatham. I've decided to ring in the New Year on my knees praying.

With time before service I stop at Destinos Mexican restaurant across the street from St. James.

It's a church that I often frequent and when no one is there, I sneak in and play the piano to the Saints.

I tell myself they like the company and they don't seem to care about my mistakes.

When I walk into Destinos I immediately feel like I'm in an episode of "The Twilight Zone." The soundtrack from *Aladdin* is playing and little kids are behind the bar.

THE NORTH

It is absolutely surreal but I decide to roll with it. "I'll have a Shirley Temple on the rocks!!"

"Coming right up," the barmaid says.

She adorns my head with a silly hat and we begin to belt out "Somebody's Got Your Back!"

My heart opens and there is a lightness that I feel in my being and as I glance at the church across the street I can't help but think that perhaps our destiny is to become like children again.

I slurp down the final drops of my Shirley Temple and high-five my new little friends. I then make my way to Payne African Methodist Episcopal Church.

It is small and humble. Run by a group of women pastors, that evoke the Spirit like I've never seen before.

I happened upon this place when I saw an advertisement for a blues performance by Rory Block.

I got this. "Yes, this is the next step in the adventure!" flutters in my heart.

So I followed the whims of my soul and let the music lead me.

Everyone this evening is dressed to impress and Reverend Gloria and Lydia greet me.

Curt gives me his warm hug, and people begin to share their gratitude for having been gifted another day.

Reverend Gloria then begins to speak about the tradition of "Watch Night" in the AME church.

I had never heard of this tradition before.

The only thing I had ever watched on New Year's was a glittery ball dropping in the middle of a neon crowd-infested Times Square.

She explains that the Watch Night service can be traced back to gatherings also known as "Freedom's Eve."

A night where black slaves and free blacks came together in churches and private homes all across the nation awaiting news that the Emancipation Proclamation actually had become law.

She tells us how at the stroke of midnight, on January 1, 1863, when all slaves in the Confederate states were declared legally free, that there were prayers and songs of joy, and people falling to their knees.

She then speaks about the history of the church.

Tells us about the time when the Ku Klux Klan set the structure that was being built on fire, and all that it has taken for them to still be standing.

The church's humble, persistent and hopeful history, remind me that this is what it means to press on.

The roof needs work. They are small in numbers, but boy are they mighty in faith.

I think of the multitudes that came before us, the interwoven narratives of our lives, the generations that came before us, and those that will come after.

It is faith like this that invigorates me. Faith like this that helps me to go on.

January 2, 2017

My friend Gabriel's mother has invited me to a New Year's women's tea and facials party at the Elixir cafe in Great Barrington.

This place seems to transport you back in time.

The wallpaper has images of life in Paris and there are porcelain teacups that make me feel like I am Alice.

I make conversation but I'm not fully there.

I can smile, talk about my plans, but I'm more concerned in engaging in a conversation with my inner world.

I thumb through some books and pull out *The Little Match Girl* by Hans Christian Andersen.

Never read it before.

It's about a little girl on a freezing New Year's Eve

Shivering, barefoot

Selling matches, and afraid to go home to an angry father

In the flame of each match that she strikes, she experiences comforting images

A holiday feast……A happy family……A shooting star

………Her grandmother

She burns more and more matches to keep the vision of her alive

Frozen, she burns the last one and is taken by her grandmother to Heaven where there is no cold, nor hunger, nor pain . . .

I burst into tears.

Gabriel's mother holds my hand. Doesn't ask for explanation.

There are some things in life that are just beyond words.

I imagine seeing my Nonna when my eyes close and I die my last death.

But I refuse to die like that match girl, with beauty, poetry, and songs still inside.

I refuse to let my light burn out that way.

No!

My spark will set this world ablaze.

January 6, 2017

I receive an email from my principal just before my first period Cultures class. It's curt and cold and it says that I should have union representation.

This can't be good. I run to tell Jake. He gives me this "did you really think this wasn't going to happen?" look.

I try to let it go and just enjoy class.

My students and I recently landed in Cuba aboard *Ms. Dina's Magic Chicken Bus* on a mission to see how studying world cultures helps us to build tolerance, enhance creativity, and solve human problems.

Seemingly idealistic, but someone needs to believe that a bunch of kids are capable of flipping the cultural iceberg, and creating peace on earth.

I greet the students at the door and with a flicker of the lights we are now in Havana.

Before beginning our tour, we give a final farewell to Bob the Balloon.

He had unfortunately gotten mauled by a gorilla after wandering off during our tour of the Kigali Genocide Museum in Rwanda, where students learned about the horrors that happen when people allow fear and hate to divide, and the magic of mercy to restore peaceful relations.

Students then listen to interviews of the Cuban people and discuss whether Castro was a "sinner, "saint", or both.

I watch enthralled by their ability to look at the totality of such a complicated figure and not succumb to clear cut dualistic judgements of "good" or "bad."

They can actually sit in the tension, a skill most adults seem to lack.

We end class with our ritualistic magic clap.

When the last child leaves, I gather myself with a few deep breaths and I walk to my principal's office in a state of dread.

We sit quietly at a round table waiting for my union rep. I pick at my nails as a way of avoiding eye contact.

When she arrives, my principal then pushes an assignment over to me that I left for my students one of the days I had called out absent.

"La Casa Ideal."

It was a short little paragraph in Spanish that I quickly wrote up with some questions attached.

The Spanish department head has circled all of my mistakes in red.

I breathe deeply.

I will not let those red marks of shame inside the chamber of my heart.

I think of my childhood home, my own "Casa Ideal" and all the cracks on my bedroom wall, which my father once painted over with vines.

I remind myself what I tell my students. "Mistakes are merely creative opportunities."

My principal then brings up a couple of absences that I didn't log using our online system.

He then calmly says, "Though it pains me to say this, I will be recommending your termination at the next board meeting."

THE NORTH

I look over at my assistant principal in utter disbelief. He holds my eye with a mix of care and guarded professionalism.

They give me an option to resign.

I try to remind myself of my spiritual principle # 12: *I look at the bright side and see the possibility in all of my experiences with an "I didn't know I wanted _____" attitude.*

"I didn't know I wanted to be fired," I repeat over and over in my head.

My union rep escorts me out of the building and I'm told to make arrangements with her to pick up my things.

I feel like Ichabod Crane being taken by the Headless Horseman.

I sit in my car in a total state of shock staring through the rainbow-colored ribbons that I bought from a street vendor at the Church of Nosso Senhor do Bonfim in Salvador.

I think about how fitting it is that the last memory I'll have in my classroom is my students packing up as Silvio Rodriguez's "Te Molesta Mi Amor" plays in the background.

Like the great troubadour, I too have that *young, maskless, bleeding, soul of everything that needs to be healed* kind of love.

If I'm honest with myself, I felt it coming. I haven't really been on my game. I've been letting go of all control in this personal experiment to see if God's plans are greater than mine.

I don't think the way I've been acting makes many people comfortable. I'm like a young Jedi warrior sloppily wielding her sword.

I try to soothe myself with Quaker talk about Way opening and closing and how sometimes our souls make the mistakes we need to usher us onto the right path.

The truth is that I am sad.

Michelle Obama is giving her farewell speech today. I wish I was at least given a chance to say goodbye.

The adventures aboard *Ms. Dina's Magic Chicken Bus* had only just begun.

There were so many more places I wanted to take them, so many cultures and people I wanted them to encounter.

I drive to St. John the Baptist's Church to pray.

I touch the painting of the Virgin of Guadalupe, recalling the day I joined the families of the students I teach on a procession of Via Crucis.

We walked three miles together that day. The women singing at the head with cute Father Dan holding the painting of the Blessed Protectress.

It was that day that I truly felt like God had brought me to this small town for a reason.

I call my friend, the matriarch of the church, the one you go to when you want to get things done. I ask if I can stop by.

All the women are making hand-made tortillas. They look at my blotchy face and ask "Que pasa Maestra?"

I tell them that I was fired and they ask if there is anything they can do.

THE NORTH

I am humbled by their offer, and tempted to put up a fight, but I feel like I need to trust that this job has been taken from me for a reason that I do not yet know.

They invite me to stay for dinner in celebration of Los Tres Reyes Magos.

I like how on this holiday little children throughout Spain and Latin America are visited by the Three Wise Men bearing gifts as if they were newborn Kings and Queens.

Italians celebrate the Epiphany with La Befana, the ancient Christmas witch who flies on her magic broom in a perpetual search for the holy child.

We rip off pieces of *rosca de reyes* bread and check to see if the baby Jesus figurine is hidden inside.

At church last week when Father Jorge had just enough figurines for every child, I jumped up like a little girl.

"It's a miracle!" I gasped.

They tell me whoever finds baby Jesus is charged with cooking tamales for the celebration of Candlemas.

Luckily for all involved, I don't find the niño Jesus in the bread, but I do think I'm starting to find him inside of me.

All the food, family, and laughter reminds me how much I miss family traditions, how much I long for my childhood home, how much I yearn to hear my Nonna and Zia Tessie harmonizing songs.

The East—
Initiation and Return Journey

Love comes with a knife
Not with some shy question
Not with fears for its reputation
Love is a mad woman, roaming the mountains
Tearing off her clothes, drinking poison
And then quietly choosing annihilation.
You have been skirting the ocean's edge
Hoisting up your robes to keep them dry
You must dive deeper, a thousand times

—Rumi

January 18, 2017

Names, Names, Names!

An alphabet soup of letters and sounds I say is me.

Dina

In Rabbi Jill Hamer's book of biblical women, the meaning of her name is endurance in spite of judgment.

Dina

She who endures . . .

Gregory

The derivative of Gregorian "to be awake," "to be watchful." The Latin form *Gregis* means "flock," "herd."

Names, Names, Names!

I have never so badly wanted to rip your last name off of me and reclaim the bloodline from which I came.

But it continues to hang like an annoying loose tooth, the kind my father used to pull in one fell swoop.

I want to be Dina Gregory again—that fighting soul whose life holds no dull moments.

Names, Names, Names!

What if, though, each letter disappeared?

First the consonants, the sharp boundaries of my identity fall one by one.

THE EAST

There goes the *d*, the *n*, the *g*, the *r*, the *y*.

I like the sound of a name composed only of melodious vowels:

Ia, Ia, Ia, Eo, Eo
Ia, Ia, Ia, Eo, Eo

A sound so soft and tender and tribal. But what if the vowels fell away?

In the stillness of silence, who AM I?

February 21, 2017

Today is our anniversary and I wonder if like me, you sometimes catch yourself looking back and wondering if things between us could be different.

Eight years ago we were getting married on that hacienda in San Miguel de Allende and today I'm standing at the edge of the sea with the world-renowned frame drummer Alessandra Belloni on the island of Oahu, Hawaii.

We make offerings of flowers to Yemaya, the Goddess of the Sea, Pele the Goddess of Volcanoes, and the Black Madonna and I can't help but feel a bit like I'm Moana

Every turn I take, every trail I track
Every path I make, every road leads back
To the place I know, where I cannot go
Though I long to be

Moana's relationship with her grandmother reminds me of my own, and that necklace Alvaro gave me that Christmas in Chile almost looks exactly the same as hers.

Perhaps our destinies are one and the same….

I wish someone would have told me a long time ago that instead of chasing prince charming, all I needed to do was go bang on a drum, reconnect with ancestral wisdom, and do MY PART to save this world with no other than empathy and love.

It makes me wonder if on those days when I feel so alone, that there isn't actually a long line of ancestors at my back cheering for me to press on.

If only I could free myself from the web of nostalgia,
perhaps then I'd truly know how far I could go?

At night we dance the ancient pizzica tarantata, a Southern Italian ritual to cure the mythological bite of love.

Writhing on the floor to the 12/8 rhythms, I allow myself to be fully taken by my own longing for the type of love, I know exists, yet feels ever so elusive.

Father Phil, an Eastern Orthodox priest who runs the farm where we've been staying has been spending the evenings teaching us about the "Sophia" or what the Greeks refer to as Wisdom….

Perhaps it is She and not He who I have been seeking all these years…

Perhaps it was HER, who I remembered in that hazy dream, on that rock in the hills of Canaan.

March 8, 2017

The piano that sits in the corner propped up against the stairwell of the community farmhouse beckons me to play it.

My fingers haven't touched the keys since I was a little girl.

My teacher Tania always said that what I lacked in technical skill I made up in soul.

She was a proud Russian woman, tall and slender with high cheekbones and ginger hair.

When I'd finish playing a song, she'd instruct me to hesitate, waiting for the lingering resonance to disappear before ceremoniously placing my hands back on my lap.

It was a fine art in and of itself.

Fingers to keys.
Keys to lap.
Fingers to keys.
Keys to lap.

Of course I didn't get it then, but I'm seeing that the seeds of wisdom that our teachers plant may take many years to sprout.

I wonder if Great Spirit can teach me how to play, can teach me how to let go of all the judgments, and help me to trust that this music already lives inside.

I imagine the Blessed Mother Mary at my side cajoling me out of my shell.

My fingers search for the chords of her sweet melancholy.

As I play, I recall my last piano recital in that Russian Orthodox Nursing Home in my little town of Nyack.

Sheer panic came over me as my mind went blank, and all I could hear was coughing.

Tania saved me, sat by my side till I could remember the song again.

Somehow I held back the tears, but as soon as I reached my father I fell into his arms and cried.

Never touched the piano keys again.

I look at the black and white keys and I give myself permission to simply let my fingers dance as they may, in search of the lost chord of grace.

I lean into the "ugly" sounds; I play them over and over again and over again, until the notions of "good" and "bad" dissolve with my loving attention.

In tears, I finally admit to myself that I am a Mystic. The prodigal daughter has returned. The violet light burns through my shame.

I can no longer deny these gifts because I am afraid to go against the grain.

I am an Artist, I admit aloud and as I hear my own voice I realize that I am becoming the woman I have always been.

I don't have paintbrushes other than the ones I carry in my mind's eye. I paint the world in the colors of the felt life.

> I am a dancer because I dance.
> I am a singer because I sing.
> I am a writer because I write.
>
> I AM that I AM!

Just like that spunky little girl from the "Soy Yo" video by Bomba Estéreo, that I taught my seventh grade Spanish class.

Cuando te critiquen, tú solo di "So Yo."

My favorite part of that music video is when that little girl with pigtails and a Band-Aid on her knee plays her plastic recorder in front of those snobby little mean girls without a care.

I still have my plastic recorder from my elementary school days.

I wonder what my music teacher, Judy Thomas, would say if she knew I spent my days playing my wooden flute to the trees.

What a teacher she was. Every day during Morning Program she had us get up on stage and we'd sing:

"Improvisation is my creation; I can do it my way, my way . . ."

Then with our hands we'd beat out a rhythm on our bodies and the entire auditorium would mimic us.

The school became a mirror of our own creation.

Ms. Thomas used to tell us that the instruments had souls, and warned us not to step over them.

She taught us African spirituals like "Wade in the Water" and that Harriet Tubman song that my friends and I from time to time still sing.

Funny how of all the things we learn and then forget, the music never dies. I remember the song like yesterday . . .

One night I dreamed.
I was in slavery 'bout 1850 was the time
sorrow was the only sign,
nothing around to ease my mind.

THE EAST

…I step away from the piano and start to rummage through the music bench.

I find a picture of Dr. King sitting atop the music sheets.

Seems an unlikely place for his photo. I feel like he is following me.

When I was at Ichabod, every time I'd go to the water fountain at school and pass his watchful eye, I couldn't shake the feeling that he was trying to tell me something.

And now of all places, I find him here.

Perhaps he is trying to tell me that his dream is part of mine and is here to remind me that I've got a ways to go before I make it to the mountain top.

I hold the picture in my hand. "What do you want from me?"

He reminds me there is no movement without music.

My heart, a drum, my breath, a song
only rhythms and wordless melodies,
no room for misinterpretation,
just sounds and colors,
and no separation.

March 16, 2017

I call you and I ask if I can drop by the farm before mass.

You open the door and I share my offering of coffee and bagels. This is us trying to be friends.

You invite me to sit down in the blue winged armchair.

I tell you about my "Spanglish" class that I've been teaching in the basement of the church and you smile as I describe old Marie's face when she recites her wild stories in Spanish.

I wish you could see the look on these women's faces when they help the English speakers pronounce words in Spanish.

There is nothing like witnessing the tables turn when the shy beginner is suddenly placed in the expert's chair.

You decide to show me a song you've been learning on the guitar. It's called "Blue Healer" by a band named Birdtalker.

You smirk when you tell me their name. There is a sweet knowing found in each other's eyes, as we soften in our shared memory of the good old times.

Like when that little city sparrow busted down the door to our home. We named him Percy, short for his persnickety ways.

I was on a camping trip with my students from Global Neighborhood Middle School in East Harlem when I got a text warning me that when I got back to our apartment that I might find a dead bird in a box.

You found him on 116th Street while walking to the subway. He was half-drowned in a puddle and you thought you would at least provide him a nice place to die.

THE EAST

I came back to find that he was very much alive.

As children both you and I had a penchant for taking care of injured birds, maybe that's why we found each other.

Percy used to greet you at the door. You'd strum your guitar and that bird and you would have a sing-along.

I never knew it, but sparrows have some serious soul.

You looked at him with a softness that I never truly got a chance to know.

Then that day came with springtime in the air that we both realized it was time to let him go.

We sat on our terrace and at first Percy wouldn't budge.

He lingered on your shoulder, taking momentary flight, not knowing nor trusting that freedom was in sight.

It's funny how the instant our attention was taken by the demands of our growling stomachs, he flew away.

The local birds made quite a racket and we looked for him for days…

I think we both are birdtalkers.

You begin to sing. Your voice is so much stronger—

> *Well the longer that you sit here lookin' into my eyes,*
> *the shock of your arrival, it begins to subside.*
> *And as I drop my defenses you start to crack a smile,*
> *are you a Blue Healer?*

A tear rolls down my cheek. I wonder if this your way of indirectly communicating with me.

When you finish, I approach you on the couch; I stroke your arm. I tell you that if you were to try, it still wouldn't be too late.

But when you don't accept my advance, I run out in a rage. I guess that song wasn't about me. What the hell is wrong with me? Why do I keep going back?

I go to the Spanish mass at St. Joseph's; I get hugs and kisses from all of my students. I smell the frankincense, feel the sun on my face as it shines through the stained glass.

Surely there must be a man who yearns to see me in full-blown color.

April 17, 2017

It's my birthday. Another year has passed. I think about how badly I want to leave my mark on this world, and yet how I also don't want to brand this Earth with another scar.

I hope that the movement of my fingers on these keys and the breath that subtly rocks this computer is a mark of my fertility.

Rock a bye baby on the tree top,
when the wind blows, the cradle will rock,
when the bough breaks
the cradle will fall, and down tumbles baby, cradle and all.

As a child my mother didn't like those lyrics, so she changed them. Who on earth would want to sing—to their young and vulnerable child—about branches breaking and babies falling?

So she'd continue on as she patted my rear end: "When the bow bends the cradle will swing and that is when Dina will hear mommy sing."

Oh, to be taught to change the words when we don't like them. It has served me well and yet it has led me to spin many lies, when reality wasn't quite matching the fantasy inside.

When I hold my mother's wrinkled hand, I know there will come a day when she too will be gone and that is certainly the day my bough will break and my cradle will fall, and down will come baby cradle and all.

The truth is that one day the branch upon which I rest will break, but why fear?

For I know in my heart that I am a songbird . . .

So move over sun and give me some sky, I've got me some wings I'm eager to fly, I may be unknown but wait till I've flown. You're gonna hear from me.

April 30, 2017

It's a sunny day in Albany and I'm in Washington Park. I have a need to be around people doing ordinary things.

There are families having picnics, and children playing tag. I hear a group of men playing the congas and I go over and begin to dance.

When I move my body and feel the sweat drip, that feeling of helplessness and loneliness fades.

There is just something in those rhythms that gives me a sense that this world can actually change.

I take a break from dancing and say hello to the group of Afghani women who are sitting at the picnic table. Their eyes caught mine as I moved and swayed.

They invite me for tea and we practice English. I think about that film at the Quaker Meeting House I recently watched called "National Bird" about the use of drone warfare in Afghanistan.

Three brave whistleblowers, who chose to listen to that small inner voice, even though their government was busy wrapping evil up in a patriotic guise of good.

I drink my tea…make funny faces at the girls.

I contemplate the ways in which my early adult life was shaped by the fall of those towers, and that email I wrote to God that night as if it were a letter to Santa…..

I prayed for us to all take pause. I prayed for my fragile heart to find the purpose in the pain.

How quick our country was to blame.

What a terrible shame that politicians do not yet know the art of lament.

The little girls follow me over to the drums. One of them marches right up to this old Puerto Rican guy and says, "I play now."

There is a fire in their eyes that gives me hope.

In a world of fearless girls, surely love will have the final say.

May 13, 2017

My Nonna. Grandmother. Sinner and Saint. Butterfly chaser, smile strewn across your face.

I still recall the way your wrinkled hands fingered your rosary beads and though they moved as you prayed there was such a solidity to your faith.

You would be proud, Nonna.

Somehow I came across a 33 day consecration to the Blessed Mother and today I have decided to give myself fully to her.

These vows make more sense to me than Buddhist refuge vows.
I can't deny my own roots. I think it's best I dig where I was planted.

Mother of us all, Mary my Queen—when I stare at that painting of you that I picked up at that record store in Hudson with the word *Whatever* inscribed on the glass in metallic paint, I get now what Julie means when she says when you embark on the initiatory journey you must commit to doing "whatever it takes."

It was right around Palm Sunday when your blue eyes caught mine.

I ran inside and joyfully asked, "How much is that Mary in the window?"

When I took that painting of you home, I took a closer look and I saw the artist's name under the metallic letter R and nearly fainted.

Florence Kroger . . .

The same artist who painted my childhood home . . .

If that isn't an apparition, I don't know what is . . .

Who needs visions when the divine reveals itself in our material world!

I begin to laugh. God has gone to such extremes to capture my attention.

All those years of being bathed in my grandmother's prayers in the tower of my childhood home in the room right next door to where my father took Grudge Records public.

Oh sweet, oh loving, oh merciful Mary, that African proverb is right

….. the medicine is next to the wound!

Even though I'm quite positive you weren't a pale white woman with blue eyes, every time I stare into them, I can't help but recall all the times shared around our family's kitchen table when my Nonna and Tess and the whole gang would harmonize songs

> *Let me call you sweetheart,*
> *I'm in love with you.*
> *Let me hear you whisper that you love me too.*
> *Keep the love light shining in your eyes so blue.*
> *Let me call you sweetheart,*
> *I'm in love with you*

God's timing is quite remarkable . . . on the anniversary of Ceil's death, and on the same day in which Pope Francis is canonizing the Fatima Seers.

My Lord, as wild and unruly as this dance of life is, there seems to be divine order to each and every single step.

I place tobacco and my grandmother's rosary beads at Mary's feet and pray.

Nonna—can you help me to trust that Creator has already choreographed the dance of my life?

Can you help me to surrender and simply follow the lead?

Nonna, do you hear me? Your prayers are being answered in unexpected ways.

Mom still suffers from hip problems. "Crack the Sky" never quite hit the billboard charts. Uncle Joey still hasn't made it rich playing the market . . .

But me, Nonna, I have faith!

And one day, I will break that stained glass ceiling so all may come to see the light!

Nonna, thank you for your prayers of intercession.

Mary, my Queen, I give unto you:

> *My eyes so that they may see your heart in that of a passing stranger,*
> *my ears so they may hear your voice in whispering winds,*
> *my hands so they may feel your touch in the embrace of a child,*
> *and my heart, so I may sing and dance in your love and light.*

Nonna, we buried your stiffened body with the Blessed Mother charm around your neck.

I questioned the logic in doing such a thing, for the soul carries nothing but its merits and good deeds, but now I see we buried a seed.......

I leave St. Mary's and drive to the re-dedication ceremony for the Persons of Color Cemetery in good ole' Kinderhook.

A group of local residents have been working on the restoration of 13 headstones in what was once an overgrown field where hundreds of African Americans were buried in the 1800's.

Curtis, from church, meets me and in the pouring rain under the tent we listen as different people speak.

A man from the Ujima Center in Albany sets the record straight that the good done was not for colored people nor slaves, but for an African people enslaved.

"One rood of land" reclaimed. Neglected stories unearthed, memory brought to light.

May 18, 2017

I'm in the city about a block away from the Fearless Girl statue when I get a call from my friend Paloma.

She tells me her uncle Waldo has died.

I can't believe what I am hearing. His wife Nury died just a little over a year ago. They have left a little girl behind.

I don't understand God sometimes. Why are they gone? Why am I here?

I recall that time when we were on vacation in Maine listening to the haunting loon calls on Twitchell Pond.

Waldo called to ask if they could stay at our apartment in Harlem so they could be near the hospital as Nury was on the brink of giving birth.

She was laying in our bathtub on 116th Street, while you and I were cuddled in bed taking turns reading excerpts from John Wellwood's book *Journey of Conscious Love*.

Back then I had no idea I'd be taking that journey alone.

I hang up with Paloma and approach the Fearless Girl statue.

I stare directly into her eyes. A group of women, with their Century 21 bags in hand, giggle as they strike a Fearless Girl pose.

My attention is then drawn to a black woman dressed in red. I walk around to get a better view.

She holds a banner that reads "In the Land of Milk & Money" and wears a bedazzled veil that says:

"She'Sus Cries"

I walk up to her and give her a hug, and feel an instant sense of relief.

Finally, someone else who gets it.

I then take a look at the Charging Bull of Wall Street and I'm flooded with memories of you.

It's Halloween; we are drunk on the subway with our friends from Spain. It is the Running of the Bulls. "Ole, Ole!"

You charge at me on the subway platform, and I'm all dressed in white with stains of Calimocho

Then I think about that Halloween when you were pepper and I was salt……

The breeze whispers, *"You are the salt of the earth…."*

Then there was that Halloween when you dressed as Wall Street and I, Main Street.

Our friend Emily stood between dressed as a gypsy with her crystal ball.

Fitting costumes, really. I'm most certainly a Main Street kind of woman.

While I can appreciate the glitter and glamor, I prefer the realness of everyday people.

May 21, 2017

I'm in a lover's apartment in Washington Heights. I met him years ago dancing forro at Mrs. Favela's in Williamsburg.

I hadn't even moved upstate yet.

I had a feeling that night when I kissed you goodnight, that I might meet someone else.

When this handsome Dominican bicyclist ended up pressing me up against the wall and kissing my neck it became hard to suppress my desire for a man to ravish me in a way in which my sensuality and sexuality could actually live together as one.

For the rest of the night, we just danced. He put me in a cab and sent me on my way.

I deleted his number from my phone and ignored him for a couple of years, trying to do what was "right."

But Life has funny ways of bringing people together again.

In bed, he hands me the trumpet sitting atop his dirty laundry basket and encourages me to give it a try.

He lets me relish in a fantasy of becoming some hot-salsa-dancing, trumpet-playing woman.

…says my thin lips are perfect for it and encourages me to take lessons.

I think about the ways in which I longed for you to encourage me in this exact way, with a wide-eyed belief in my ability to do anything I put my mind to.

But of course, you and I speak different love languages.

THE EAST

I'd write you beautiful love notes and encourage your many latent talents and you'd fill my tires with air, patiently fix my parents' computer, and ensure that the ins and outs of daily life functioned like a well-oiled machine.

No wonder our *love tanks always ran on empty.*

Naked in my lover's arms, I sound the trumpet and he looks at me with fascination.

"*Ay Mira como lo tocas. Eres un natural.*" He is probably putting me on, but I like it.

I giggle thinking that this would be a pretty funny way for God to have someone sound the last trumpet.

On his wall are pictures of Che Guevara, Simon Bolivar, and other Latin American liberators.

I momentarily imagine myself as Dina La Libera in a sexy fatigue dress, and an army of dancers behind me liberating the world one dance at a time.

I must admit that lately my imagination has been on overdrive. I think I probably have been watching too much *Jane the Virgin.*

When I leave his apartment, I stop to call my mom to share with her the latest happenings of my romantic life and a misspelled Bible quote from Matthew 5:44 – 48, that someone had taped on a traffic divider, catches my eye.

It reads, "But I say unto you, love your enemies, bless them that curse you, do good to them that hate you, and pray for them which despitefully use you, and persecute you. In Yeshua's name, Amen. Jesus *love* you."

That third person singular 's' is difficult for my students whose first language is not English. It's not Jesus love you. It's Jesus *loves* you. Funny but I'm starting to actually believe that is true.

June 2, 2017

I've been teaching a journalism class twice a week to third graders at Hudson Elementary School and it's got me yearning to go back to a world of lost innocence.

Peter, the man who hired me, likes to talk about observable facts. We differ quite a bit on our philosophy of education but we both seek solace in the quiet of the Victory Chapel at Our Lady's feet.

I confide in him a lot about my divorce. I send him long and winding disjointed narratives trying to make sense of the breakdown of my marriage as it is juxtaposed against the breakdown of our democracy.

He tells me that he is a journalist, not a therapist. He tells me to keep the faith and that he has been praying for me to just say "The End," and move on with my life.

But I don't know how to say "The End." Literature has clear beginnings and endings, but life?

How do you say "The End" when the legend is still being lived?

We debate a lot about the acquisition of knowledge and he likes to make fun of my whimsical flights of imagination.

So what if I dream of a world where the unicorns and fairies return to assist us in remembering our shared humanity?

I want less complicated thoughts, more curiosity, and a whole lot of magic in my life.

I'm done with losing myself in apocalyptic prophecies of doom and gloom; I want to lose myself in love.

When class starts, I have the kids stand and I let the Mary Poppins in me out.

"Okay kids—two turns to the right, and one turn to the left!"

Poof! Now a third grader is a journalist.

Is that all it takes to leave it all behind, and become someone new.

Two turns to the right, and one turn to the left.

"Careful," I warn them. "If you do it in the reverse direction you might end up turning into a porcupine."

I teach them the magic reverse blink, the one my best friend and I read about in Douglas Coupland's book *Life after God*.

They close their eyes, then open them briefly, and take a picture with their mind's eye.

My best friend Beverly and I savored that book during a summer backpacking trip in Europe.

We'd sit on benches with a bottle of warm wine and take turns reading each other our favorite lines.

She read an excerpt from it on our wedding day.

Every time I turn its pages, I am reminded that all of CREATION speaks.

Everything I touch, every lyric I hear, every book I read

—there seems to be a bit of truth hidden in all things.

June 22, 2017

The Quaker community discerned that they wouldn't be renewing my lease.

I've got to admit the timing of it felt like a low blow.

Between death, divorce, getting fired, and then being told that it is best for me and for them if I move on, it hit upon my deepest wound; my fear that I don't belong.

We had several Care Committee meetings in typical Quaker fashion. It was a helpful space to process my feelings and prepare myself for yet another transition.

I get it God. It's all temporary. I'm but a mere pilgrim. You've made your point.

It's funny that as soon as I begin to feel at home, life brings change.

I guess this is what it means to feel like a fox without a foxhole, stumbling along.

I'm in Boston now living in a dancer's artist collective, mentoring young teens about the power of salsa music to bring people together and transform communities.

Above my new bedroom door is a decal that says "Home is where the heart is." It is a not an easy lesson to learn.

I saw a picture of you and your new girlfriend on Facebook.

I guess moving on has been made official. I watch as you two replay scenes from the days of *our* lives.

A trip to meet your parents.
An afternoon of Chihuly Gardens and Glass.
A day spent betting the ponies at the track.

Then of course that scene where we marvel at the peeps of the baby barn swallows and later walk hand in hand, stopping to greet the pig guy from Lover's Leap Farm.

I feel replaced.

Like an entire part of my life has been left on the cutting room floor and I've been cast away on the lone isle of my heart.

Yes, I have taken to Instagram stalking. Seeing her sitting in the corner where I spent my mornings with pen in hand I have a sudden urge to fight you for our sacred land.

But what good would that be? Is not every bit of earth upon which my feet kiss considered holy?

This thread of faith is all that remains.

My housemate Katie and I drive to a salsa event we are producing and we blast Kesha's new song "Praying."

When I listen to it, I realize that though at times I think I'm special, this journey I'm on is not so unique.

We search for soul mates and end up with wound mates.

Life brings us to a point where we find ourselves alone, beaten down, broken, forced to surrender to a force much greater than ourselves.

I hope you're somewhere prayin', prayin'
I hope your soul is changin', changin'
I hope you find your peace
Falling on your knees, prayin'

THE EAST

As the light turns red, I catch a glimpse of a bronze angel on a building ledge, poking through the leafy trees and I know you see me, God, even when I don't feel seen.

We are at another traffic light across from a bar named Phoenix Landing.

A girl wearing a red polka-dotted dress passes by and I recall that threshold upon which I laid down my polka-dotted dream, and where I made that promise to keep moving East.

It would have been nice if after completing my year of Initiation, I could have put my feet up and said that I had somehow arrived.

But this Wheel I see is more of a spiral, and with each turn we are brought to greater depths.

Our event is in an outdoor park. We lay the dance floor in the drizzling rain and I catch a glimpse of a Betty Boop sticker on a nearby car.

She winks at me. Tells me to look up and I realize I'm standing in front of the Church of Transfiguration.

Maybe that is what I am here to do. To dance myself into a being of light.

Could it really be that simple?

To spend my days giving God my praise through song and dance.

June 24, 2017

I am celebrating the solstice at Soul Fire Farm.
The woman on the mic pours libations to the ancestors,
recalling mothers who braided seeds of hope in their hair before boarding transatlantic slave ships.

I can hardly imagine that kind of faith:
To hold onto a dream in spite of all odds,
that one day your children will reap what you have sown.

She invites us to call out to our ancestors in unison.
I call out to my Nonna.
I speak her name and we bow and pray.
a spirit of justice and defiant joy pervades
as we dance the night away.

September 11, 2017

Words.
You are daggers that pierce the skin,
exposing that we are mere mortals,
finite beings of blood and bones . . .
but my dreams,
they are eternal ones.

I struggle, though.
There are so many directions I'm pulled in,
and time keeps ticking.
and the sands keep passing through the hourglass.

As my neighbor Derrick likes to say, "It's got me goin' like an octopus on roller skates."

But lying down in my bed, the noise in my head begins to subside, and in the whispering wind I hear my Queen say:

"Let go AND let be. Just breathe. A dreamer's job is to simply dream."

September 26, 2017

My father and I take a drive to our spot on Harrier Hill. I crack open a Coors Light and we drink a beer, staring at the Catskill Mountains.

The goldenrod sways before us and it is apparent that there is something quite mystical about this land of love and lore.

Tomorrow he has surgery and it's got me scared that this moment could be our last.

I wonder . . . if something happened, if I would regret all the stories of his days in the music business that I still can't recall no matter how many times he tries to tell them to me?

It makes me sad that he doesn't see himself as a success.

Without his ear, there is so much music this world may never have come to know.

While I may not be able to recall the details of his career, I know I will never forget this moment.

Yes. This Moment!

Out beyond the hills where Rip Van Winkle once awoke, I too am now AWAKE and I recall that we are all mere seedfolks in God's KINdom.

Seedfolks- that book has been a touchstone of my teaching practice.

It's a story about one little girl who planted but a mere seed of her father's in some dirty lot of land and created a slice of Heaven right here on Earth.

THE EAST

As I gaze upon this field of glory, I can't help but to smirk. All these years seeking God in far off and distant lands, and I come to find the Father sitting next to you.

October 5, 2017

Life has brought me back full circle and I'm living again in Harlem about twenty-five blocks from where we first lived.

Every end a new beginning, every beginning a new end. . .

I got a job at Bronx International High School. I'm on the Metamorphosis team and I'm teaching a class called Reading and Discourse to beginning ESL students from the Dominican Republic and several countries in West Africa.

The building is a castle and I feel like a princess in a never-ending tale.

Our department head has given me a banner to decorate my classroom with. It says: "Be curious, explore ideas, make connections, share new understandings, and discover yourself."

I find myself staring at it a lot. Is that really what this entire journey is all about?

Is this what Baldwin meant when he said that an artist is a sort of emotional and spiritual historian?

> *Oh the doom and the glory of knowing who you are.*

With political divisions, racism, sexism, militarism, and climate change, there are days when my entire being succumbs to these apocalyptic narratives of "End Times". I can hardly move from my bed overtaken by the grief of our nuclear apathy.

But I'm starting to have faith the size of a mustard seed that the Joseph Campbell quote that hangs just above the secretary's desk is right.

"Just when the caterpillar thought the world was over, he became a butterfly"

THE EAST

I guess patience is a virtue because Metamorphosis takes time.

November 13, 2017

I found a church for the time being where my Soul unexpectedly feels at home, a place where I don't feel like I have to hide my feelings, in fear of being "too much."

Mother Zion on 137th Street.

The numbers are dwindling, but Soul is clearly alive.

The lace curtains in the music room remind me of the ones my mother had in her bedroom of my childhood home.

And that altar feels like it can hold every joy and every pain of my raptured Soul.

Sojourner Truth and Frederick Douglass were members here.

It is steeped in a history that I do not fully know, yet I can't help but feel drawn by the collective yearning for liberation that this space holds.

I guess I too am a sojourner of sorts. A wanderer searching for the lost keys to freedom.

I get all weepy when we sing to the congregation and the mix of international guests about "how easy it is to love."

I often stare at the stained glass window of mother and holy child, wondering why that which is so easy, is also so hard?

Why do we resist surrendering our hearts to God's outpouring of mercy, grace, and love?

Do we fear that all the illusions we've built our lives upon will be burned?

Do we fear that we might be swept away by the tragic beauty of it all?

> Blessed Mother
> Help me to have faith
> Help me to trust
> Help me to dispel the fear,
> And accept that your grace is enough.

November 16, 2017

I stand in the center of the Rivers Cosmogram, at the Schomburg Center

The ashes of Langston Hughes beneath my feet, and I must admit, that my soul, too, has grown deep like the rivers.

Mahicantuck
River That Flows Both Ways

Early sailors called you the "World's End." But, I call you my Lonely Girl.

I set a goldfish free on your banks, holding my grandmother's hand, gifted the river with flowers for the Goddess Oshun.

I wept sorrowful tears on the beaches where the *Half Moon* once sailed, as I read my lonely girl a children's book called *The People Shall Continue*.

As a teenager, I sat watching the rising tide contemplating all the twists and turns my life would take.

Wondered if there was another soul in the world who could understand the intensity that I feel coursing through the blood in my veins.

My soul, too, has grown deep like the rivers . . .

Maya Angelou once danced upon this very spot. No better way for the living to honor the dead than to dance our prayers and gift the Earth with our beads of sweat.

It makes me think that those *djembes* I heard in the City of Lights on my sweet sixteen, that drew me to them like a moth to a flame, really do talk.

And that love story that I caught a glimpse of in that puddle on the cobblestone street in Paris ……..was actually my own.

My soul, too, has grown deep like the rivers . . .

And as I stand in the center of this Cosmogram, Creator's masterpiece unfolds before my watchful eye.

And I see that I am nothing more than my search history.

Chispa417, a divine spark. My blood an inheritance of ancient pasts, and modern times.

A weaver of worlds, a bridge between the seen and unseen

My soul, too, has grown deep like the rivers . . .

December 22, 2017

It's International Day at school and we are celebrating with song, dance, and copious amounts of food.

Olivier and I joyfully bust out some dance moves as the students look on.

He and I have been working on a little creative writing project that he decided to take on after our class finished reading a beginner-friendly version of "The Legend of Sleepy Hollow."

All the kids had a fit when Katrina ended up choosing Brom Bones and poor Ichabod was taken by the Headless Horseman, leaving all the townspeople to wonder about the fate of that quirky schoolteacher.

"*Coño, no es justo*," one student shouted.

Olivier said he didn't like the ending either, so I encouraged him to change it.

It's funny how life works. The lessons I am called to teach are the ones I actually need to learn the most.

I forget that I too have the power to grab a pen, flip the script, and with the help of God write my world anew.

In his version, when Ichabod is thrown from his horse, he ends up in a magical portal and is woken up by a bunch of fishermen in Burkina Faso who nurse him back to health.

The fishermen bring him to the chief, and the villagers rejoice at his surprisingly good dance moves.

He doesn't know it, but his imagination is restoring the remaining pieces of my broken heart. And though life and love is ever-unfolding, it's clear the time has finally come to say……….

THE EAST

"The End"

. . . I broke free from the chains of the marrying maiden. Awoke on a rock in the hills of Canaan. In Harlem, I was lost and found.

The silver lining of my pain reveals itself in a painting of divine lovers propped up against a liquor store on Lenox Avenue.

A woman named Smurf with a scar on her face is my witness, as the seed of a mystical marriage is planted in the bridal chamber of my heart.

The outer? Nothing more than a reflection of the inner . . .

And I want to proclaim from every hilltop, that I believe in an evolutionary kind of love.

The kind of love that's not formed in a quick storm of passion.

No, but the kind that slowly percolates, until it dawns upon you that in your quest to find "the one," He's been there all along.

Standing at your side peering inside your shy soul, hunting you down and you didn't even know.

I believe in an evolutionary kind of love. The kind of love created in the Heavens where Me becomes We.

Head in the clouds, feet on the ground, the Earth trembles with our sacred intention.

I believe in an evolutionary kind of love, like the parable of the boiling frog, the kind of love that slowly brings upon the death of all illusion.

The kind of love the world has been waiting on. It is time for the King and Queen, to take their rightful place inside the church of my winged body, for I am the bride and it is time for the Sheep to become one Fold.

Listen to yourself and in that quietude you might hear the voice of God.
—*Maya Angelou*

Wedding Day, February 21st, 2009

Afterword

I am often asked about the ring that you see on the cover of this book. After my divorce was finalized, I was quite adamant that before even thinking about getting remarried to another man, I would first and foremost marry my Soul.

    I suggested to a friend of mine that he should hide a ring for me and the day I found it would signify that my Soul had proposed to me. I never gave him a ring to hide and yet my Soul still found a way.

    One afternoon as I was walking around my neighborhood in Harlem, I stopped at the John Paul II Senior Complex. I was drawn by a wooden sign called "JD's Crafts" and a large dollhouse that stood at the entrance of the gate.

    JD was the name of me and my ex-husband's stuffed rooster who used to come on all of our trips. Naturally this sign caught my eye. Within a few minutes JD ran up to me and proudly told me that the entire dollhouse was made with sticks that you can find in your kitchen. The dollhouse, including all of its furniture, took him three years to make, about the same amount of time it took for me to make a home in my own body.

    As I was marveling at all the tiny pieces of handmade furniture, I suddenly felt a tap on my shoulder. I turned around and found him on one knee with a ring made of popsicle sticks and the remnants of an old earring. He jokingly asked if I would marry him. I laughed. Of course my Soul would propose to me this way!

AFTERWORD

When I wear this ring, I am reminded of the ways in which the old can be made new, the powers of destruction and creation, and most importantly that the only wedding that truly leads to "happily ever after" is the sacred inner marriage.

Three months after receiving my "engagement ring," I travelled to Southern Italy on a pilgrimage of the Black Madonna with world-renowned healer and frame drummer Alessandra Belloni.

A friend of mine told me before my trip that I was about to be step into Act IV and he was right. The inner sacred marriage that I had experienced inside the chamber of my heart, was seemingly brought to life during the Feast of the Madonna in Seminara, Calabria.

Giant puppets paraded around the streets. They were meant to represent the folkloric story of the African king falling in love with the Italian princess, and the Black Madonna, known as Our Lady of the Poor, bringing people together in love, equality, and compassion.

Hearing the sound of those drums in my own ancestral land while staring at those giant puppets, I was reminded of my wedding at that hacienda in San Miguel de Allende, and the giant papier-mâché mojigangas of the bride, groom, and the Lady in Red.

In that moment my entire journey of conscious love made complete and utter sense. The passion I had been seeking with a man would never satiate the depths of my spiritual thirst. It was only in the realization of my Oneness in Christ, Sophia, and all of Creation that could cure the pain of unrequited love, the loneliness and longing for a home to which I cannot return, and the grief for the lost people and places of my past.

When I witnessed the reenactment of this folkloric wedding, I realized that this was the love that I set out to find when I laid my marriage down on that threshold and made my commitment to keep moving East.

Seeing this wedding reflected before me on the stage of life, I realized in that moment that Kahil Gibran's poem "On Marriage" that my Aunt Ardie read on our wedding on February 21, 2009, was right. We cannot make a bond of love "for only the hand of life can contain your heart."

Since then I sold my fancy engagement ring and wedding band. I no longer have a coconut band hidden in a porcelain box in the back of a dresser drawer. I keep it front and center on my altar and I give thanks for simplicity and all the relationships both romantic and platonic that have revealed to me that the "KINdom" of God, is in fact, right on here on earth.

Since then I have realized that Pope Francis is correct in saying that "the church isn't an institution but a love story," one that I contend we are still living out, for the ultimate marriage is not one that binds two people, but one that unites the Soul with the world.

*

I'm dancing everywhere in the streets.
When I climb this mountain,
I will dance higher and higher on the mountain,
and when I get to the top,
I'll start dancing even more and more and more and more.
At the top, I'll sing my song, my favorite song.
Swing around the mountain hill.
Swing around the mountain hill.
And when I dance around
I'll have that great old feeling again.

Acknowledgments

First and foremost, I want to thank my Nonna Anna and all of my ancestors; Mary, my Queen, and all of my guides both known and unknown. Thank you for helping me to blaze my own path.

Mom and Dad. You have cheered me on my entire life, and have been there for me through both the joy and the pain. Though it pains me to watch you grow old, it is through your love that I have learned the enduring and merciful love of our Divine Father and our dear Mother Earth.

Joseph. Thank you for the years we spent together—the good, the bad, and the ugly. I am sorry you got the worst of me and not the best. I wish you and your family nothing short of the best.

Ceil. Your death made me awaken to the truth of my life. Thank you for teaching me that one can be a mother without having children. Thank you for saving my life when I choked on a Dorito, and the ways in which you visit me in images of Betty Boop.

Don. I never thought I would be able to say your name without saying Ceil's. You have stood by my side all these years as I've walked through grief to find my joy. You have taught me that in life the only path is forward.

Alvaro. I have learned from you that there are certain relationships that bust down the door to your soul. You certainly did that for me, opening me to a world of passion that without you I would never have known.

Julie Tallard Johnson. Thank you for being a real spiritual teacher without all the B.S., for telling it like it is and giving me the compass that helped me navigate my way to my true Self.

Elana Bell. Thank you for encouraging the sacred creative in me.

Audrey Dimola. Wildlight. Thank you for living your legend.

Anne Dillon. Thank you for your tender and loving edits and helping to see myself and my writing in a new light.

Marie Claude. I sat next to you at the Omega Institute because I wanted to sing the blues and you helped me discover the mystic artist that I am. Thank you for listening to your own intuition and showing up when I was most in need.

Alessandra Belloni. Thank you for following the music and the call of the Black Madonna. You have played and continue to play an integral role in re-connecting me to my ancestral roots.

Quaker Intentional Village-Canaan (QIVC) Family. Thanks for holding my heart in the light. You taught me that spirituality is at the end of the day very simple. Sit in silence, listen to the teacher within, and take care of your neighbor.

St. Joseph's Church. Thank you to the beautiful and humble Souls—especially to the Spanish speaking community whose deep adoration for the Virgin of Guadalupe brought me back to the roots of my own faith.

Payne AME. Your faith, your welcoming ways, your deep wisdom. Thank you for teaching me that small can be mighty.

Mother Zion AME. Thank you for your help in my journey in finding my voice and making me feel welcome and at home.

The Gathering Harlem. Thank you for reminding me that roses can grow from concrete.

Worshipful Praises Dance Ministry- Thanks for the sisterhood.

ACKNOWLEDGMENTS

And to the many other communities both spiritual and secular in nature that have left their mark on my soul.

To the family, friends, lovers, teachers and students that I have not named; thank you for being a part of my ever-unfolding journey.

To the prophets dressed in rags, and to the children whose innocence reminds me what it means to be a child of God.

To all of my relations.

By virtue of my efforts, may all beings be freed from the bonds of mental slavery.

May we receive that which we need to fulfill our earthly needs and the tools to tend to the gardens of our Souls.

As we journey through this circle of life, may we continually move Eastward bringing forth the vision contained within the rising sun.

And as we do so, may the glory of God be revealed through the expression of human goodness.

Made in the USA
Middletown, DE
18 February 2020